First International Workshop on Natural Language Processing Beyond Text (NLPBT 2020)

Online
20 November 2020

ISBN: 978-1-7138-1999-8

NLPBT 2020

NLP Beyond Text

**Proceedings of the First International Workshop on
Natural Language Processing Beyond Text**

November 20, 2020
Online

Introduction

Humans interact with each other through several means (e.g., voice, gestures, written text, facial expressions, etc.) and a natural human-machine interaction system should preserve the same modality. However, traditional Natural Language Processing (NLP) focuses on analyzing textual input to solve language understanding and reasoning tasks, and other modalities are only partially targeted. This workshop aims to promote research in the area of Multi/Cross-Modal NLP, i.e., studying computational approaches exploiting the different modalities humans adopt to communicate. In particular, the focus of this workshop is (i) studying how to bridge the gap between NLP on spoken and written language and (ii) exploring how NLU models can be empowered by jointly analyzing multiple input sources, including language (spoken or written), vision (gestures and expressions) and acoustic (paralingustic) modalities. The former comes from the observation that voice-based interaction, which is typical of conversational agents, poses new challenges to NLU. The latter aims to address the way humans acquire and use language. Usually, it happens in a perceptually rich environment, where they communicate using modalities that go beyond language itself. Therefore, extending NLP to modalities beyond written text is a fundamental step in allowing AI systems to reach human-like capabilities.

Organizers:

Giuseppe Castellucci, Amazon
Simone Filice, Amazon
Soujanya Poria, Singapore University of Technology and Design
Erik Cambria, Nanyang Technological University
Lucia Specia, University of Sheffield

Program Committee:

Sawsan Alqahtani, George Washington University
Udit Arora, New York University
Loïc Barrault, University of Sheffield
Emanuele Bastianelli, Philips
Raffaella Bernardi, University of Trento
Fethi Bougares, University of Le Mans
Ozan Caglayan, Imperial College London
Marcus Collins, Amazon
Danilo Croce, University of Roma Tor Vergata
Jean-Benoit Delbrouck, Stanford University
Asif Ekbal, Indian Institute of Technology Patna
Marina Fomicheva, University of Sheffield
Alexander Gelbukh, Instituto Politécnico Nacional
Md Kamrul Hasan, Bangladesh University of Engineering and Technology
Sudipta Kar, Amazon
Penny Karanasou, Amazon
Aman Khullar, IIIT Hyderabad
Samira Korani, Sharif University
Paul Pu Liang, CMU
Jindřich Libovický, Charles University
Shervin Malmasi, Amazon
Elman Mansimov, New York University
Wasifur Rahman, University of Rochester
Akhilesh Ravi, Indian Institute of Technology Gandhinagar
Anna Rohrbach, UC Berkeley
Salvatore Romeo, Amazon
Ramon Sanabria, University of Edinburgh
Sonal Sannigrahi, Ecole Polytechnique
Ranjan Satapathy, Nanyang Technological University
Tejas Srinivasan, Carnegie Mellon University
Umut Sulubacak, University of Helsinki
Shuai Tang, University of California, San Diego
Noé Tits, University of Mons
Kohei Uehara, University of Tokyo
Andrea Vanzo, Sinequanon
Chao Wang, University of Southern California

Invited Speaker:

Loïc Barrault, University of Sheffield

Table of Contents

Program

November 20, 2020

15:00 - 15:10 UTC   **Opening NLPBT**

15:10 - 16:10 UTC   **Session: Session A**

15:10 UTC
Modulated Fusion using Transformer for Linguistic-Acoustic Emotion Recognition
Jean-Benoit Delbrouck, Noé Tits and Stéphane Dupont

15:30 UTC
Multimodal Speech Recognition with Unstructured Audio Masking
Tejas Srinivasan, Ramon Sanabria, Florian Metze and Desmond Elliott

15:50 UTC
EMNLP Findings Paper 1
TBA

16:10 - 17:00 UTC   **Keynote**

16:10 UTC
A Vision on (Simultaneous) Multimodal Machine Translation
Loïc Barrault

17:00 - 18:30 UTC   **Session: Poster Session**

Building a Bridge: A Method for Image-Text Sarcasm Detection Without Pretraining on Image-Text Data
Xinyu Wang, Xiaowen Sun, Tan Yang and Hongbo Wang

A Benchmark for Structured Procedural Knowledge Extraction from Cooking Videos
Frank F. Xu, Lei Ji, Botian Shi, Junyi Du, Graham Neubig, Yonatan Bisk and Nan Duan

A Multi-Modal English-Italian Parallel Corpus for End-to-End Speech-to-Text Machine Translation
Giuseppe Della Corte and Sara Stymne

Unsupervised Keyword Extraction for Full-Sentence VQA
Kohei Uehara and Tatsuya Harada

18:30 - 19:50 UTC	**Session: Session B**

18:30 UTC   *MAST: Multimodal Abstractive Summarization with Trimodal Hierarchical Attention*
Aman Khullar and Udit Arora

18:50 UTC   *Towards End-to-End In-Image Neural Machine Translation*
Elman Mansimov, Mitchell Stern, Mia Chen, Orhan Firat, Jakob Uszkoreit and Puneet Jain

19:10 UTC   *EMNLP Findings Paper 2*
TBA

19:30 UTC   *Reasoning Over History: Context Aware Visual Dialog*
Muhammad Shah, Shikib Mehri and Tejas Srinivasan

19:50 - 20:00 UTC   **Closing NLPBT**

The EMNLP Findings papers will be announced on https://sites.google.com/view/nlpbt-2020

Modulated Fusion using Transformer for Linguistic-Acoustic Emotion Recognition

Jean-Benoit Delbrouck
Stanford University
jeanbenoit.delbrouck@stanford.edu

Noé Tits and **Stéphane Dupont**
Information, Signal and Artificial Intelligence
University of Mons, Belgium
{noe.tits, stephane.dupont}@umons.ac.be

Abstract

This paper aims to bring a new lightweight yet powerful solution for the task of Emotion Recognition and Sentiment Analysis. Our motivation is to propose two architectures based on Transformers and modulation that combine the linguistic and acoustic inputs from a wide range of datasets to challenge, and sometimes surpass, the state-of-the-art in the field. To demonstrate the efficiency of our models, we carefully evaluate their performances on the IEMOCAP, MOSI, MOSEI and MELD dataset. The experiments can be directly replicated and the code is fully open for future researches[1].

1 Introduction

Understanding expressed sentiment and emotions are two crucial factors in human multimodal language yet predicting affective states from multimedia remains a challenging task. The emotion recognition task has existed working on different types of signals, typically audio, video and text. Deep Learning techniques allow the development of novel paradigms to use these different signals in one model to leverage joint information extraction from different sources. These models usually require a fusion between modality, a crucial step to compute expressive multimodal features used by a classifier to output probabilities over the possible answers.

In this paper, we propose an architecture based on two stages: an independent sequential stage based on LSTM (Hochreiter and Schmidhuber, 1997) where modality features are computed separately, and a second hierarchical stage based on Transformer (Vaswani et al., 2017) where we iteratively compute and fuse new multimodal representations. This paper proposes the fusion between the

acoustic and linguistic features through attention modulation (Yu et al., 2019) and linear modulation (Dumoulin et al., 2018), a powerful tool to shift and scale the feature maps of one modality given the representation of another.

The association of this horizontal-vertical encoding and modulated fusion shows really strong results across a wide range of datasets for emotion recognition and sentiment analysis. In addition to the interesting performances it offers, the modulation requires no or very few learning parameters, making it fast and easy to train. The paper is structured as follows: we first present the different researches used for comparison in our experiments in section 2, we then briefly present the different datasets in section 3. Then we carefully describe our sequential feature extraction based on LSTM in section 4 and the two hierarchical modulated fusion model, the Modulated Attention Transformer (MAT) and Modulated Normalization Transformer (MNT), in section 5. Finally, we explain the experimental settings in section 6 and report the results of our model variants in section 7.

2 Related Work

The presented related work is used for comparison for our experiments. We proceed to briefly describe their proposed models.

First, Zadeh et al. (2018b) proposed a novel multimodal fusion technique called the Dynamic Fusion Graph (DFG) to study the nature of cross-modal dynamics in multimodal language. DFG contains built-in efficacies that are directly related to how modalities interact.

To capture the context of the conversation through all modalities, the current speaker and listener(s) in the conversation, and the relevance and relationship between the available modalities through an adequate fusion mechanism, Shenoy

---

[1] https://github.com/jbdel/modulated_fusion_transformer

1

Proceedings of the First International Workshop on Natural Language Processing Beyond Text, pages 1–10
Online, November 20, 2020. ©2020 Association for Computational Linguistics
http://www.aclweb.org/anthology/W23-20%2d

and Sardana (2020) proposed a recurrent neural network architecture that attempts to take into account all the mentioned drawbacks, and keeps track of the context of the conversation, interlocutor states, and the emotions conveyed by the speakers in the conversation.

Pham et al. (2019) presented a model that learns robust joint representations by cyclic translations between modalities (MCTN), that achieved strong results on various word-aligned human multimodal language tasks.

Wang et al. (2019) proposed the Recurrent Attended Variation Embedding Network (RAVEN) to model expressive nonverbal representations by analyzing the fine-grained visual and acoustic patterns that occur during word segments. In addition, they seek to capture the dynamic nature of nonverbal intents by shifting word representations based on the accompanying nonverbal behaviors.

But the related work that is probably the closest to ours is the Multimodal Transformer (Tsai et al., 2019; Delbrouck et al., 2020) because they also use Transformer based solutions to encode their modalities. Nonetheless, we differ in many ways. First, their best solutions and scores reported are using visual support. Secondly, they use Transformer for cross-modality encoding for every modality pairs; this equals to 6 Transformer modules (2 pairs per modality) while we only use two Transformer (one per modality). Finally, each output pairs is concatenated to go though a second stage of Transformer encoding. We also differ on how the features are extracted: they base their solution on CNN while we use LSTM. In this paper, it is important to note that we compare our results to their word-unaligned scores, as we do not use word-alignment either.

3 Datasets

3.1 IEMOCAP dataset

IEMOCAP (Busso et al., 2008) is a multimodal dataset of dyadic conversations of actors. The modalities recorded are Audio, Video and Motion Capture data. All conversations were segmented, transcribed and annotated with two different emotional types of labels: emotion categories (6 basic emotions (Ekman, 1999) – happiness, sadness, anger, surprise, fear, disgust – plus frustrated, excited and neutral) and continuous emotional dimensions (valence, arousal and dominance).

For categorical labels, the annotators could also select "other" if they found the emotion could not be described with one of the adjectives. The categorical labels were given by 3-4 evaluators. Majority vote was used to have the final label. In case of ex aequo, it was considered not consistent in terms of inter-evaluator agreement; 7532 segments out of the 10039 segments reached agreement.

To be comparable to previous research, we use the four categories: neutral, sad, happy, angry. Happy category is obtained by merging excited and happy labeled (Yoon et al., 2018), we obtain a total of 5531 utterances: 1636 happy, 1084 sad, 1103 angry, 1708 neutral. The train-test split is made according to Poria et al. (2017) as it seems to be the norm for recent works.

3.2 CMU-MOSI dataset

CMU-MOSI (Zadeh et al., 2016) dataset is a collection of video clips containing opinions. The collected videos come from YouTube and were selected with metada using the #vlog hashtag for *video-blog* which desribes a specific type of video that often contains people expressing their opinion. The resulting dataset included clips with speakers with different ethnicities but all speaking in english. The speech was manually transcribed. These transcriptions were aligned with audio at word level. The videos were annotated in sentiment with a 7-point Likert scale (from -3 to 3) by five workers for each video using Amazon's Mechanical Turk.

3.3 CMU-MOSEI dataset

MOSEI (Zadeh et al., 2018c) is the next generation of MOSI dataset. They also took advantage of online videos containing expressed opinions. They analyzed videos with a face detection algorithm and selected videos with only one speaker with an attention directed to the camera.

They used a set of 250 different keywords to scrape the videos and kept a maximum of 10 videos for each one with manual transcription included. The dataset was then manually curated to keep only data with good quality. It is annotated with a 7-point Likert scale as well as the six basic emotion categories (Ekman, 1999).

3.4 MELD dataset

The Multimodal EmotionLines Dataset (MELD) (Poria et al., 2019) contains dialogue instances that encompasses audio and visual modality along with text. MELD has more than 1400 dialogues and 13000 utterances from Friends TV series. Multiple speakers participated in the dialogues. Each utterance in a dialogue has been labeled by any of these seven emotions: Anger, Disgust, Sadness, Joy, Neutral, Surprise and Fear. MELD also has sentiment (positive, negative and neutral) annotation for each utterance.

4 Feature extractions

This sections aims to describe the linguistic and acoustic features used as the input of our proposed modulated fusions based on Transformers. The extraction is performed independently for each sample of a dataset. We denote the extracted linguistic features as x and acoustic as y. In the end, both x and y have a size $[T, C]$ where T is the temporal axis size and C the feature size. Its important to note that T is different for each sample, while C is a hyper-parameter.

4.1 Linguistic

A sentence is tokenized and lowercased. We remove special characters and punctuation. We build our vocabulary against the train-set of the datasets and embed each word in a vector of 300 dimensions using GloVe (Pennington et al., 2014). If a word from the validation or test-set is not in present our vocabulary, we replace it with the unknown token "unk". Each sentence is run through an unidirectional one-layered LSTM of size C. The size of each linguistic example x is therefore $[T, C]$ where T is the number of words in the sentence.

4.2 Acoustic features

In the litterature of multimodal emotion recognition, many works use hand designed acoustic features sets that capture information about prosody and vocal quality such as ComPaRe (Computational Paralinguitic Challenge) feature sets from Interspeech conference.

However, with the evolution of deep learning models, lower level features such as mel-spectrograms have shown to be very powerful for speech related tasks such as speech recognition and speech synthesis. In this work we extract mel-spetrograms with the same procedure as a typical seq2seq Text-to-Speech system.

Specifically, our mel-spectrograms were extracted with the same procedure as in (Tachibana et al., 2018) with librosa python library (McFee et al., 2015) with 80 filter banks (the embedding size is therefore 80). A temporal reduction is then

applied by selecting one frame every 16 frames. Each spectrogram is then run through an unidirectional one-layered LSTM of size C. The size of each acoustic example y is therefore $[T, C]$ where T is the number of frames in the spectrogram.

5 Models

This section aims to describe the three model variants evaluated in our experiments. First, we describe the projection (P) of the features extracted in section 4 over emotion and sentiment classes without using any Transformer. This corresponds to the baseline for our experiments. Secondly, we present the Naive Transformer (NT) model, a transformer-based encoding where the inputs are encoded separately, the linguistic and acoustic features do not interact with each other: there is no modulated fusion. Finally, we present the two highlights of the paper, the Modulated Attention Transformer (MAT) and the Modulated Normalization Transformer (MNT), two solutions where the encoded linguistic representation modulates the entire process of the acoustic encoding.

5.1 Projection

Given the linguistic features x and acoustic features y extracted at section 4, we define the projection as a two-step process. First, we use an attention-reduce mechanism over each modality, and then fuse both modality vectors using a simple element-wise sum.

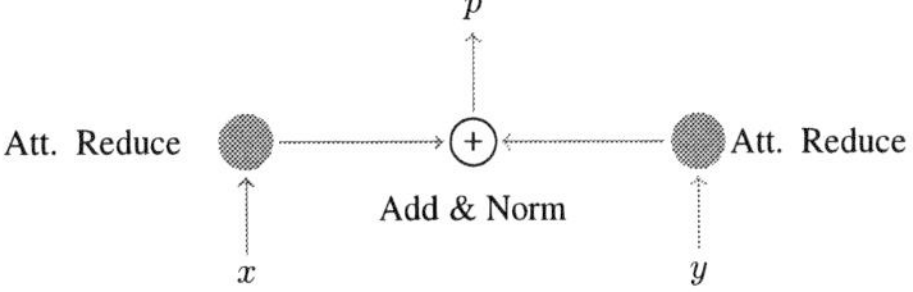

Figure 1: Projection

The attention-reduce mechanism consists of a soft-attention over itself followed by a weighted-sum computed according to the attention weights. If we consider the feature input x of size $[T, C]$:

$$a_i = \mathrm{softmax}(v_i^{a\top}(W_x x))$$
$$\bar{x} = \sum_{i=0}^{T} a_i x_i \tag{1}$$

After this reduce mechanism, the input becomes vectors of size $[1, C]$. We can then apply the element-wise sum as follows:

$$y \sim p = W_p(\text{LayerNorm}(\bar{x} + \bar{y})) \qquad (2)$$

where p is the distribution of probabilities over possible answers and LayerNorm denotes Layer Normalization (Ba et al., 2016). If we assume the input feature x has the shape $[T, C]$, for each feature channel $c \in \{1, 2, \cdots, C\}$

$$\mu_{i,c} = \frac{1}{T} \sum_{t=1}^{T} x_{i,t,c}$$

$$\sigma_{i,c}^2 = \frac{1}{T} \sum_{t=1}^{T} (x_{i,t,c} - \mu_{i,c})^2 \qquad (3)$$

$$\hat{x}_{i,t,c} = \frac{x_{i,t,c} - \mu_{i,c}}{\sqrt{\sigma_{i,c}^2}}$$

Finally, for each channel, we have learnable parameters γ_c and β_c, such that:

$$y_{i,:,c} = \gamma_c \hat{x}_{i,:,c} + \beta_c \qquad (4)$$

5.2 Naive Transformer

The Naive Transformer model consists of stacking a Transformer on top of the linguistic and acoustic features extracted at section 4 before the projection of section 5.1. Transformers are independent and their respective input features do not interact with each other.

A Transformer is composed of a stack of B identical blocks but with their own set of training parameters. Each block has two sub-layers. There is a residual connection around each of the two sub-layers, followed by layer normalization (Ba et al., 2016). The output of each sub-layer can be written like this:

$$\text{LayerNorm}(x + \text{Sublayer}(x)) \qquad (5)$$

where Sublayer(x) is the function implemented by the sub-layer itself. In traditional Transformers, the two sub-layers are respectively a multi-head self-attention mechanism and a simple Multi-Layer Perceptron (MLP).

The attention mechanism consists of a Key K and Query Q that interacts together to output a attention map applied to Value V:

$$\text{Attention}(Q, K, V) = \text{softmax}\left(\frac{QK^\top}{\sqrt{C}}\right) V \qquad (6)$$

In the case of self-attention, K, Q and V are the same input. If this input is of size $T \times C$, the operation $QK^\top$ results in a squared attention matrix containing the affinity between each row T. Expression $\sqrt{C}$ is a scaling factor. The multi-head attention (MHA) is the idea of stacking several self-attention attending the information from different representation sub-spaces at different positions:

$$\text{MHA}(Q, K, V) = \text{Concat}(\text{head}_1, ..., \text{head}_h)W_o$$
$$\text{where head}_i = \text{Attention}(QW_i^Q, KW_i^K, VW_i^V) \qquad (7)$$

A subspace is defined as slice of the feature dimension k. In the case of four heads, a slice would be of size $\frac{k}{4}$. The idea is to produce different sets of attention weights for different feature sub-spaces. In the context of Transformers, Q, K and V are x for the linguistic Transformer and y for the acoustic Transformer. Throughout the MHA, the feature size of x and y remains unchanged, namely C.

The MLP consists of two layers of respective sizes $[C \rightarrow \overline{C}]$ and $[\overline{C} \rightarrow C]$. After encoding through the blocks, the outputs $\tilde{x}$ and $\tilde{y}$ can be used by the projection layer (section 5.1) for classification. In Figure 2, we show the encoding of the linguistic features x and its corresponding output $\tilde{x}$.

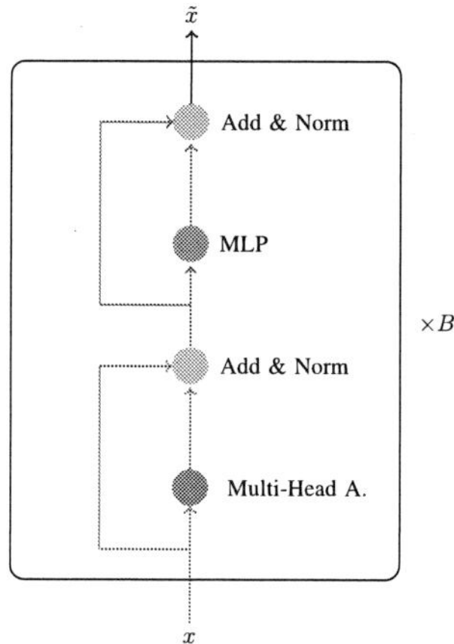

Figure 2: Linguistic Naive Transformer.

5.3 Modulated Fusion

The Modulated Fusion consists of modulating the encoding of the acoustic features y given the encoded linguistic features $\tilde{x}$. This modulation in the acoustic Transformer allows for an early fusion of both modality whose result is going to be $\tilde{y}$. This modulation can be performed through the Multi-Head Attention or the Layer-Normalization. After, the output $\tilde{x}$ and $\tilde{y}$ are used as input of the projection from section 5.1. We proceed to describe both approaches in the next sub-sections.

5.3.1 Modulated Attention Transformer

To modulate the acoustic self-attention by the linguistic output, we switch the key K and value V of the self-attention from y to $\tilde{x}$. The operation $QK^{\top}$ results in an attention map that acts like an affinity matrix between the rows of modality matrix $\tilde{x}$ and y. This computed alignment is applied over the Value V (now $\tilde{x}$) and finally we add the residual connection y. The following equation describes the new attention sub-layer in the acoustic Transformer.

$$y = \text{LayerNorm}(y + \text{MHA}(y, x, x)) \quad (8)$$

For the operation $QK^{\top}$ to work as well as the residual connection (the addition), the feature sizes C of $\tilde{x}$ and y must be equal. This can be adjusted with the different transformation matrices of the MHA module or the LSTM size of section 4.

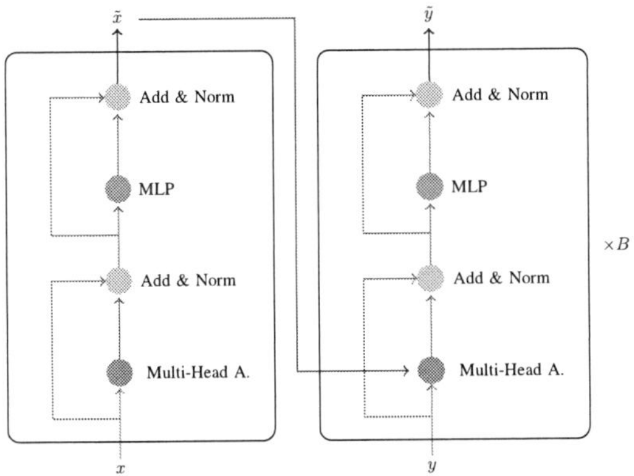

Figure 3: Modulated Attention Transformer.

If we consider that $\tilde{x}$ is of size $[T_x, C]$ and y of size $[T_y, C]$, then the sizes of the matrix multiplication operations of this modulated attention can be written as follows (where $\times$ denotes matrix multiplication):

$$y \times x^T = T_y, C \times C, T_x = T_y, T_x \quad (9)$$
$$(9) \times x = T_y, T_x \times T_x, C = T_y, C \quad (10)$$
$$(10) + y = T_y, C + T_y, C = T_y, C \quad (11)$$

where equation 11 denotes the $(y + \text{MHA}(y, x, x))$ operation.

We call the Modulated Attention Transformer "MAT" in the experiments.

5.3.2 Modulated Normalization Transformer

It is possible to modulate the normalization layers by predicting two scalars per block from $\tilde{x}$, namely $\Delta\gamma$ and $\Delta\beta$, that will be added to the learnable parameters of equation 4:

$$\begin{aligned} \overline{\gamma_c} &= \gamma_c + \Delta\gamma \\ \overline{\beta_c} &= \beta_c + \Delta\beta \end{aligned} \quad (12)$$

where $\Delta\gamma$, $\Delta\beta = \text{MLP}(\tilde{x})$ and the MLP has one layer of sizes $[C, 4 \times B]$. Two pairs of scalars per block are predicted, so no scalars are shared amongst normalization layers.

We update the layer normalization equation accordingly:

$$y_{i,:,c} = \overline{\gamma_c}\hat{x}_{i,:,c} + \overline{\beta_c} \quad (13)$$

The Modulated Normalization is a computationally efficient and powerful method to modulate neural activations. It enables the linguistic output to manipulate entire acoutisc feature maps by scaling them up or down, negating them, or shutting them off. As there is only two parameters per feature map, the total number of new training parameters is small. This makes the Modulated Normalization a very scalable method.

We call the Modulated Normalization Transformer "MNT" in the experiments.

6 Experimental settings

We train our models using the Adam optimizer (Kingma and Ba, 2014) with a learning rate of $1e - 4$ and a mini-batch size of 32. If the accuracy score on the validation set does not increase for a given epoch, we apply a learning-rate decay of factor 0.5. We decay our learning rate up to 2 times. Afterwards, we use an early-stop of 10 epochs on accuracy. Results presented in this paper are from the averaged predictions of at most 10 models.

Unless stated otherwise, the LSTM size C (and therefore the Transformer size) is 512. We use $B = 2$ Transformer blocks for P and NT models and $B = 4$ for MNT and MAT models. We use 8 multi-heads regardless of the models or the modality encoded. The size $\overline{C}$ of the Transformer MLP is set at 2048. We apply dropout of 0.1 on the output of each block iteration, and 0.5 on the input $(x + y)$ of the projection layer (equation 2).

7 Results

We present the results on four sentiment and emotion recognition datasets: IEMOCAP, MOSEI, MOSI and MELD. For each dataset, the results are presented in terms of the popular metrics used for the dataset. Most of the time, F1-score is used, and sometimes the weighted F1-scores to take into account the imbalance between emotion or sentiment classes.

IEMOCAP We first compare the precision, recall and unweighted F1-scores of our two model variants on IEMOCAP in Table 3. We notice that our MAT model comes on top.

Model	Prec.	Recall	F1
MAT (L+A, ours)	**0.74**	**0.74**	**0.74**
MNT (L+A, ours)	0.72	0.72	0.72
NT (L+A, ours)	0.71	0.70	0.70
P (L+A, ours)	0.69	0.67	0.67
Mult (L+A+V, 2019)	-	-	0.715
E2 (L+A, 2019)	0.73	0.715	0.72
MDRE (L+A, 2018)	0.72	-	-
MDREA (L+A, 2018)	0.69	-	-
E1 (L+A, 2019)	0.73	0.655	0.68
RAVEN, (L+A+V, 2019)	-	-	0.665
MCTN, (L, 2018)	-	-	0.66

Table 1: Results of the 4-emotions task of IEMOCAP. Prec. stands for precision and F1 is the unweighted F1-score.

If we compare the F1-score per class (table 2), we notice that our model MAT outperforms previous researches, the biggest margin being in the happy category. The model MulT (Tsai et al., 2019) still comes on top in the neutral category.

Model	Hap.	Ang.	Sad	Neu.	avg
MAT (ours)	**0.68**	**0.71**	**0.75**	0.80	**0.73**
MNT (ours)	0.66	**0.71**	0.72	0.80	0.72
NT (ours)	0.67	0.69	0.69	0.78	0.70
P (L+A, ours)	0.63	0.65	0.68	0.78	0.67
MulT (2019)	0.60	0.70	0.74	**0.82**	0.71
MCTN (2018)	0.49	0.66	0.72	0.78	0.66
RAVEN (2019)	0.60	0.64	0.66	0.77	0.66

Table 2: IEMOCAP: F1-scores per emotion class. Avg denotes the weighted average F1-score.

We can see in Figure 4 that our MNT model has a really good recall on the neutral category but MAT significantly outperforms MNT in the happy cateogry. However, we can see that the happy class surprisingly remains a challenge for the models presented. Our MAT model predicted around 17% of the time "angry" when the true class was happy. On the contrary, our model predicted "happy" 19% of the time when the true label was "sad" and 17% of the time when the true class was "angry". We can see that this is still a significant margin of error for such contradictory labels. It shows that visual cues might be necessary to further improve the performances.

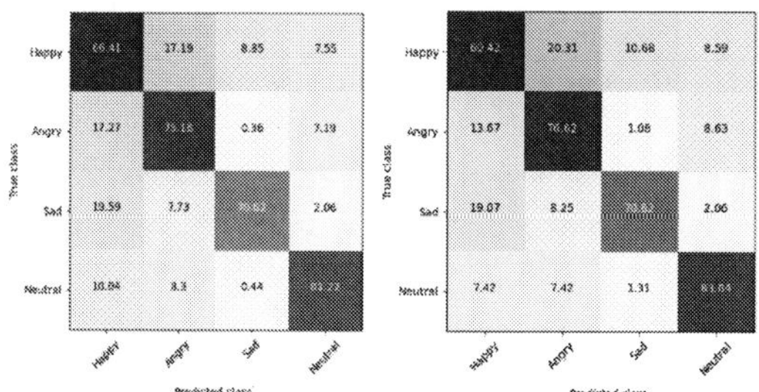

Figure 4: Confusion matrices for IEMOCAP emotion task.

MOSI MOSI is a small dataset with few training examples. To train such models, regularization is usually needed to not overfit the training-set. In our case, dropout was enough to top the state-of-the-art results on this dataset.

Even if the dataset is a bit unbalanced between the binary answers (positive and negative), weighting the loss accordingly did not improve the results. It shows that our model variants manage to efficiently discriminate between both classes.

Model	F1
MAT (L+A, ours)	0.80 (0.84 / 0.73)
MNT (L+A, ours)	0.80 (0.84 / 0.73)
NT (L+A, ours)	0.78 (0.83 / 0.71)
P (L+A, ours)	0.76 (0.80 / 0.71)
MulT (L+A+V, 2019)	**0.81**
SA-Gating B6 (L+A+V, 2020)	**0.81**
Multilogue-Net (L+A+V, 2020)	0.80
Multilogue-Net (L+A, 2020)	0.79

Table 3: Results on the 2-sentiment task of MOSI. Results given are the weighted F1-scores.

MOSEI MOSEI is a relatively large-scale dataset. We expect to see a more noticeable difference of score between our Modulated Transformer variants and the Naive Transformer and Projection baselines.

For the emotion task in Table 4, MNT comes on top with a noticeable improvement over the state-of-the-art in the Surprise and Fear category.

Model	Happy	Sad	Angry
MNT (ours)	0.66	**0.76**	0.77
MAT (ours)	0.66	0.75	0.75
NT (ours)	0.65	0.75	0.74
M-logue (2020)	**0.68**	0.75	**0.81**
G-MFN (2018b)	0.66	0.67	0.73
Model	Fear	Disgust	Surprise
MNT (ours)	**0.92**	0.85	**0.91**
MAT	0.91	0.84	0.89
P (ours)	0.88	0.84	0.86
Multilogue	0.87	**0.87**	0.81
G-MFN	0.79	0.77	0.85

Table 4: Results on the 6-emotions classification task of MOSEI. Metrics reported are the weighted F1-scores. M-logue stands for Multilogue-Net and G-MFN for Graph-MFN.

Multilogue still shows strong results in the Happy and Angry category, two important classes of the MOSEI dataset as they have the biggest support (respectively 2505 and 1071 samples over 6336 in the test-set). For binary sentiment classification (Table 5), MAT is the strongest reported model.

Model	A2	F1
MAT (L+A, ours)	**0.82**	**0.82**
MNT (L+A, ours)	0.805	0.805
NT (L+A, ours)	0.81	0.80
P (L+A, ours)	0.805	0.79
MulT (L+A+V, 2019)	0.815	0.815
RAVEN (L+A+V, 2019)	0.79	0.795
G-MFN (L+A+V, 2018b)	0.79	-
MCTN (L, 2019)	0.75	0.76

Table 5: Results on the 2-sentiments task of MO-SEI. Results given are the accuracies and weighted F1-scores.

MELD   MELD is a dataset for Emotion Recognition in Conversation. Even if our approaches do not take into account the context, we can see that it leads to interesting results. More precisely, our variants are able to detect difficult emotion, such as fear and disgust, even though they are present in very low quantity in the training and test-set.

We can see in Table 6 that even if we do not use the contextual nor the speaker information, our models achieve good results in two categories: fear and disgust. To help understand these results, we give two MELD examples in Figure 5. In the top example, it is unlikely to answer "anger" to the

sentence "you fell asleep!" without context, it could be surprise or fear. This is why our "anger" score is really low. In the bottom example, "you have no idea how loud they are" could very well be "anger" too, but happens to be labeled "disgust".

Model	Ang.	Dis.	Fear	Joy
MNT (ours)	0.27	**0.21**	**0.12**	0.41
MAT (ours)	0.27	0.15	0.09	0.42
NT (ours)	0.25	0.11	0.05	0.39
CGCN*† (2019)	**0.47**	0.11	0.09	0.53
DRNN* (2019)	0.46	0.0	0.0	0.53
BC-LSTM*	0.46	0.0	0.0	0.50
G-MFN (2018a)	0.40	0.0	0.0	0.47
Model	Neut.	Sad	Surp.	
MNT (ours)	0.66	0.24	0.46	
MAT (ours)	0.63	0.22	0.44	
NT (ours)	0.54	0.21	0.41	
GCN*†	**0.77**	**0.28**	0.50	
DRNN*	0.73	0.25	**0.52**	
BC-LSTM*	0.76	0.16	0.48	
G-MFN	0.76	0.13	0.41	

Table 6: Results of the 7-emotions (Anger, Disgust, Fear, Joy, Neutral, Sad, Surprise) task of MELD. Results given in term of F1-scores. DRNN is DialogueRNN, G-MFN is Graph-MFN and CGCN is ConGCN. * denotes that a model uses the contextual information and † speaker information.

It is possible that our model, without any prior or contextual bias about an utterance, classify sentences similar to "you fell asleep" or "you have no idea how" as "disgust" or "fear". Further analysis on why our model perform so well could shed the light on this odd behavior. We also fall short on the sad and surprise category compared to GCN, showing that a variant of our proposed models that takes into account the context could lead to competitive results.

8   Further analysis

A few supplementary comments can be made about the results. First, we notice that the hierarchical structure of the network brought by the transformers did bring improvements across all datasets. Indeed, even the NT model does bring significant performances boost compared to the P model that only consists of an LSTM and the projection layer. A very nice property of our solutions is that few Tranformers layers are required to be the found settings. It usually varies from 2 to 4 layers, allowing our solutions to converge very rapidly.

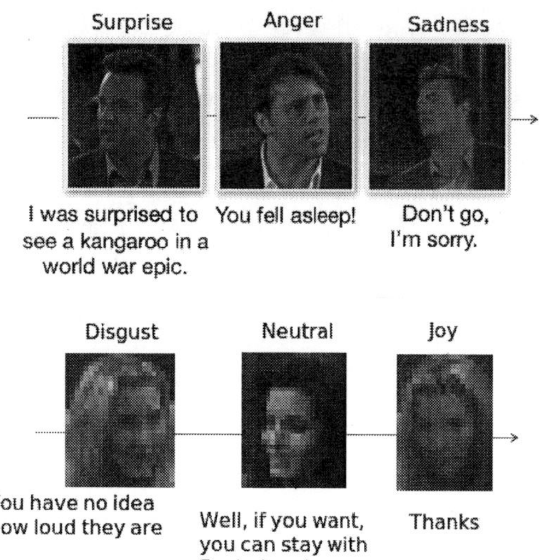

Figure 5: MELD: Two contextual examples with three training samples each.

MOSEI	Params	s/epoch	epoch/c
P	9.8 M	10	2
NT $B = 2$	22.9 M	26	6
NT $B = 4$	35.5 M	42	7
MAT $B = 2$	22.9 M	26	8
MAT $B = 4$	35.5 M	42	10
MNT $B = 2$	24.5 M	26	6
MNT $B = 4$	39.9 M	44	8

Table 7: Results on a single GTX 1080 Ti for $C = 512$. The statistics reported are from the MOSEI dataset for the sentiment task, as it contains the most training samples (16320). s/epoch means seconds per epoch and epoch/c means the number of epoch to convergence. Parameters are reported in Million.

Another point is that the MAT variant does not require additional training parameters nor computational power (as shown in Table 7), the solution only switch one input of the Multi-Head Attention from one modality matrix to another. For MNT, the Transformer block implements only 2 normalization layers, therefore the conditional layer must only compute 2048 scalars (given C is 512) for $\Delta\gamma$ and $\Delta\beta$ or roughly 1 Million parameters per block. This solution grows linearly with the hidden size but we got better results with $C = 512$ rather than 1024.

The difference between MAT and MNT variant is slim, but it seems that MAT is more suitable for the binary sentiment classification. The computed alignment by the modulated attention of the linguistic and acoustic modality proves to be an acceptable solution for 2-class problem, but seems to fall short for more nuanced classification such as multi-class emotion recognition. MNT seems more suitable for that task, as shown for MOSEI and MELD. A potential issue for MAT is that we work with shallow architectures ($B = 4$) compared to recent NLP solutions like BERT using up to 48 layers. In the scope of the dataset presented, we have not enough samples to train such architectures. It is possible that MNT adjust better with shallow layers because it can modulate entire feature maps twice per blocks.

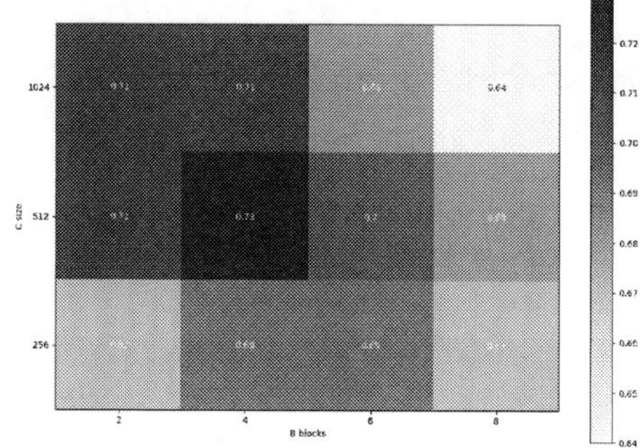

Figure 6: Heatmap showing the influence on f1-scores from parameters B and C on IEMOCAP.

9 Conclusions

In this paper, we propose two different architectures, MAT (Modulated Attention Transformer) and MNT (Modulated Normalization Transformer), for the task of emotion recognition and sentiment analysis. They are based on Transformers and use two modalities: linguistic and acoustic.

The performance of our methods were thoroughly studied by comparison with a Naive Transformer baseline and the most relevant related works on several datasets suited for our experiments.

We showed that our Transformer baseline encoding separately both modalities already performs well compared to state-of-the-art. The solutions including modulation of one modality from the other show a higher performance. Overall, the architectures offer an efficient, lightweight and scalable solution that challenges, and sometimes surpasses, the previous works in the field.

Acknowledgements

Noé Tits is funded through a FRIA grant (Fonds pour la Formation à la Recherche dans l'Industrie et l'Agriculture, Belgium).

References

Jimmy Lei Ba, Jamie Ryan Kiros, and Geoffrey E Hinton. 2016. Layer normalization. *arXiv preprint arXiv:1607.06450.*

Carlos Busso, Murtaza Bulut, Chi-Chun Lee, Abe Kazemzadeh, Emily Mower, Samuel Kim, Jeannette N Chang, Sungbok Lee, and Shrikanth S Narayanan. 2008. Iemocap: Interactive emotional dyadic motion capture database. *Language resources and evaluation*, 42(4):335.

Jean-Benoit Delbrouck, Noé Tits, Mathilde Brousmiche, and Stéphane Dupont. 2020. A transformer-based joint-encoding for emotion recognition and sentiment analysis. In *Second Grand-Challenge and Workshop on Multimodal Language (Challenge-HML)*, pages 1–7, Seattle, USA. Association for Computational Linguistics.

Vincent Dumoulin, Ethan Perez, Nathan Schucher, Florian Strub, Harm de Vries, Aaron Courville, and Yoshua Bengio. 2018. Feature-wise transformations. *Distill.* Https://distill.pub/2018/feature-wise-transformations.

Paul Ekman. 1999. Basic emotions. *Handbook of cognition and emotion*, 98(45-60):16.

Sepp Hochreiter and Jürgen Schmidhuber. 1997. Long short-term memory. *Neural computation*, 9(8):1735–1780.

Diederik P Kingma and Jimmy Ba. 2014. Adam: A method for stochastic optimization. *arXiv preprint arXiv:1412.6980.*

Ayush Kumar and Jithendra Vepa. 2020. Gated mechanism for attention based multi modal sentiment analysis. In *ICASSP 2020-2020 IEEE International Conference on Acoustics, Speech and Signal Processing (ICASSP)*, pages 4477–4481. IEEE.

Navonil Majumder, Soujanya Poria, Devamanyu Hazarika, Rada Mihalcea, Alexander Gelbukh, and Erik Cambria. 2019. Dialoguernn: An attentive rnn for emotion detection in conversations. In *Proceedings of the AAAI Conference on Artificial Intelligence*, volume 33, pages 6818–6825.

Brian McFee, Colin Raffel, Dawen Liang, Daniel PW Ellis, Matt McVicar, Eric Battenberg, and Oriol Nieto. 2015. librosa: Audio and music signal analysis in python. In *Proceedings of the 14th python in science conference*, pages 18–25.

Jeffrey Pennington, Richard Socher, and Christopher D Manning. 2014. Glove: Global vectors for word representation. In *EMNLP*, volume 14, pages 1532–1543.

Hai Pham, Paul Pu Liang, Thomas Manzini, Louis-Philippe Morency, and Barnabás Póczos. 2019. Found in translation: Learning robust joint representations by cyclic translations between modalities. In *Proceedings of the AAAI Conference on Artificial Intelligence*, volume 33, pages 6892–6899.

Hai Pham, Thomas Manzini, Paul Pu Liang, and Barnabás Poczós. 2018. Seq2Seq2Sentiment: Multimodal sequence to sequence models for sentiment analysis. In *Proceedings of Grand Challenge and Workshop on Human Multimodal Language (Challenge-HML)*, pages 53–63, Melbourne, Australia. Association for Computational Linguistics.

Soujanya Poria, Erik Cambria, Devamanyu Hazarika, Navonil Majumder, Amir Zadeh, and Louis-Philippe Morency. 2017. Context-dependent sentiment analysis in user-generated videos. In *Proceedings of the 55th annual meeting of the association for computational linguistics (volume 1: Long papers)*, pages 873–883.

Soujanya Poria, Devamanyu Hazarika, Navonil Majumder, Gautam Naik, Erik Cambria, and Rada Mihalcea. 2019. Meld: A multimodal multi-party dataset for emotion recognition in conversations. In *Proceedings of the 57th Annual Meeting of the Association for Computational Linguistics*, pages 527–536.

Gaurav Sahu. 2019. Multimodal speech emotion recognition and ambiguity resolution. *arXiv preprint arXiv:1904.06022.*

Aman Shenoy and Ashish Sardana. 2020. Multiloguenet: A context aware rnn for multi-modal emotion detection and sentiment analysis in conversation. *arXiv preprint arXiv:2002.08267.*

Hideyuki Tachibana, Katsuya Uenoyama, and Shunsuke Aihara. 2018. Efficiently trainable text-to-speech system based on deep convolutional networks with guided attention. In *2018 IEEE International Conference on Acoustics, Speech and Signal Processing (ICASSP)*, pages 4784–4788. IEEE.

Yao-Hung Hubert Tsai, Shaojie Bai, Paul Pu Liang, J. Zico Kolter, Louis-Philippe Morency, and Ruslan Salakhutdinov. 2019. Multimodal transformer for unaligned multimodal language sequences. In *Proceedings of the 57th Annual Meeting of the Association for Computational Linguistics (Volume 1: Long Papers)*, Florence, Italy. Association for Computational Linguistics.

Ashish Vaswani, Noam Shazeer, Niki Parmar, Jakob Uszkoreit, Llion Jones, Aidan N Gomez, Łukasz Kaiser, and Illia Polosukhin. 2017. Attention is all you need. In *Advances in neural information processing systems*, pages 5998–6008.

Yansen Wang, Ying Shen, Zhun Liu, Paul Pu Liang, Amir Zadeh, and Louis-Philippe Morency. 2019. Words can shift: Dynamically adjusting word representations using nonverbal behaviors. In *Proceedings of the AAAI Conference on Artificial Intelligence*, volume 33, pages 7216–7223.

Seunghyun Yoon, Seokhyun Byun, and Kyomin Jung. 2018. Multimodal speech emotion recognition using audio and text. In *2018 IEEE Spoken Language Technology Workshop (SLT)*, pages 112–118. IEEE.

Zhou Yu, Jun Yu, Yuhao Cui, Dacheng Tao, and Qi Tian. 2019. Deep modular co-attention networks for visual question answering. In *Proceedings of the IEEE Conference on Computer Vision and Pattern Recognition*, pages 6281–6290.

Amir Zadeh, Paul Pu Liang, Navonil Mazumder, Soujanya Poria, Erik Cambria, and Louis-Philippe Morency. 2018a. Memory fusion network for multi-view sequential learning. In *Thirty-Second AAAI Conference on Artificial Intelligence*.

Amir Zadeh, Rowan Zellers, Eli Pincus, and Louis-Philippe Morency. 2016. Mosi: multimodal corpus of sentiment intensity and subjectivity analysis in online opinion videos. *arXiv preprint arXiv:1606.06259*.

AmirAli Zadeh, Paul Pu Liang, Soujanya Poria, Erik Cambria, and Louis-Philippe Morency. 2018b. Multimodal language analysis in the wild: CMU-MOSEI dataset and interpretable dynamic fusion graph. In *Proceedings of the 56th Annual Meeting of the Association for Computational Linguistics (Volume 1: Long Papers)*, pages 2236–2246, Melbourne, Australia. Association for Computational Linguistics.

AmirAli Zadeh, Paul Pu Liang, Soujanya Poria, Erik Cambria, and Louis-Philippe Morency. 2018c. Multimodal language analysis in the wild: CMU-MOSEI dataset and interpretable dynamic fusion graph. In *Proceedings of the 56th Annual Meeting of the Association for Computational Linguistics (Volume 1: Long Papers)*, pages 2236–2246, Melbourne, Australia. Association for Computational Linguistics.

Dong Zhang, Liangqing Wu, Changlong Sun, Shoushan Li, Qiaoming Zhu, and Guodong Zhou. 2019. Modeling both context-and speaker-sensitive dependence for emotion detection in multi-speaker conversations. In *Proceedings of the 28th International Joint Conference on Artificial Intelligence*, pages 5415–5421. AAAI Press.

Multimodal Speech Recognition with Unstructured Audio Masking

Tejas Srinivasan
Language Technologies Institute
Carnegie Mellon University
tsriniva@andrew.cmu.edu

Ramon Sanabria
CSTR, ILCC
University of Edinburgh
r.sanabria@ed.ac.uk

Florian Metze
Language Technologies Institute
Carnegie Mellon University
fmetze@andrew.cmu.edu

Desmond Elliott
Department of Computer Science
University of Copenhagen
de@di.ku.dk

Abstract

Visual context has been shown to be useful for automatic speech recognition (ASR) systems when the speech signal is noisy or corrupted. Previous work, however, has only demonstrated the utility of visual context in an unrealistic setting, where a fixed set of words are systematically masked in the audio. In this paper, we simulate a more realistic masking scenario during model training, called Rand-WordMask, where the masking can occur for any word segment. Our experiments on the Flickr 8K Audio Captions Corpus show that multimodal ASR can generalize to recover different types of masked words in this unstructured masking setting. Moreover, our analysis shows that our models are capable of attending to the visual signal when the audio signal is corrupted. These results show that multimodal ASR systems can leverage the visual signal in more generalized noisy scenarios.

1 Introduction

Jointly modelling linguistic and visual signals is beneficial for several language processing tasks, such as machine translation (Sulubacak et al., 2019), visual question-answering (VQA) (Antol et al., 2015), summarization (Palaskar et al., 2019) and automatic speech recognition (ASR) (Palaskar et al., 2018; Sanabria et al., 2018). However, it is unclear exactly how the visual signals are useful for these tasks. For example, in VQA, it has been observed that models can ignore the visual context and instead rely on linguistic biases in the dataset (Ramakrishnan et al., 2018; Grand and Belinkov, 2019); in machine translation, it has been shown that some models are not affected by incorrect visual signals (Elliott, 2018); and in multimodal ASR, the visual signals were shown to act as a regularizer instead of useful disambiguating context (Caglayan et al., 2019). Given these uncer-

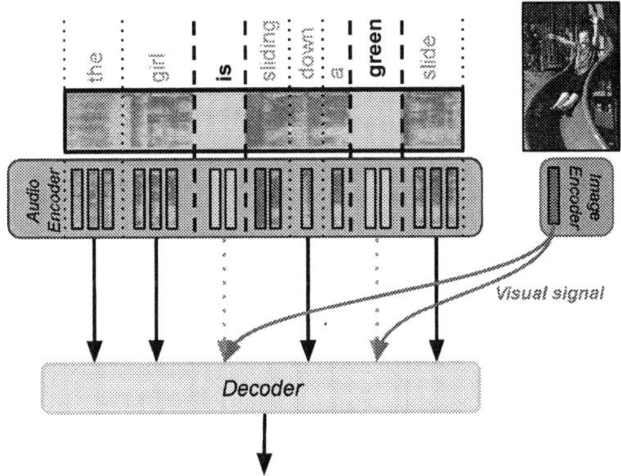

Figure 1: We propose to train multimodal speech recognition models while randomly masking different types of words in the speech signal. The model learns to use the visual signal to correctly predict the masked words.

tainties, there is a need to clarify the circumstances in which visual signals are useful.

Previous work in multimodal machine translation (Caglayan et al., 2019) and ASR (Srinivasan et al., 2020) shows that the visual signal is useful when the linguistic signal is degraded by dropping the input. In this setting, multimodal models leverage the visual signals to recover the missing language information. The results in (Srinivasan et al., 2020) are a promising start towards *verifiably useful* multimodality for robust speech recognition. However, the experiments were conducted with structured noise that focused on a predetermined set of groundable entities (*i.e.*, nouns and places). In real world scenarios, however, noise occurs in a more unstructured manner. Therefore, it is important that multimodal models can use the visual signal in a wider variety of situations.

In this work, we study multimodal ASR in more realistic noisy scenarios. We follow the methodology from (Srinivasan et al., 2020) but we randomly

11

Proceedings of the First International Workshop on Natural Language Processing Beyond Text, pages 11–18
Online, November 20, 2020. ©2020 Association for Computational Linguistics

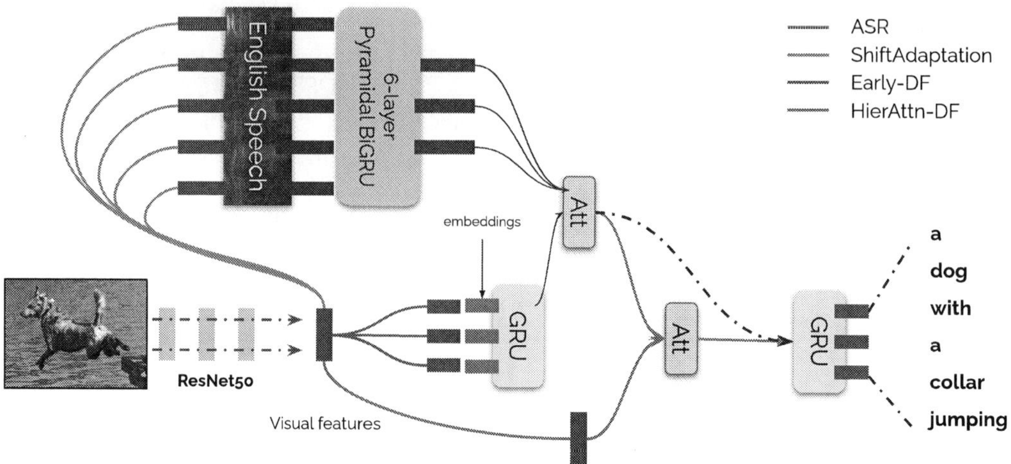

Figure 2: Our unimodal ASR model, along with several of our fusion methods for integrating a visual context vector (in blue) into the ASR model. The two fusion methods not displayed above, Weighted-DF and Middle-DF, were constructed similar to Early-DF and HierAttn-DF respectively

mask words in an unstructured manner in the audio signal (we refer to this as RandWordMask). This is in contrast to the structured masking in (Srinivasan et al., 2020), where the masked audio corresponds to only entities (which we refer to as EntityMask). The example in Figure 1 shows that RandWordMask can mask any words in the audio signal, whereas EntityMask would only mask entities like "girl" and "slide". We apply masking both during training and testing.

The main contributions of this work are:

- We simulate a more realistic masking scenario, called RandWordMask[1], during training and testing of our ASR models (Section 2).

- We propose several multimodal models (Section 2.2), and show that training with RandWordMask improves their ability to recover masked words (Section 4).

- We show that our multimodal ASR models are right for the right reasons through several quantitative analyses (Section 4.1, 4.2, 4.4).

The results show that visual signals improve speech recognition in this more difficult, unstructured setting where random words are masked. Our models are not only able to recover masked entities, but they also recover words from other syntactic

categories, *e.g.*, adjectives, cardinals, and verbs. Furthermore, our analysis shows that our models when trained using RandWordMask attend to the visual signal when the audio signal is unavailable. This confirms that the visual context can be leveraged when the primary audio signal is masked.

2 Methodology

In this section, we describe the different ASR models and our technique for simulating unstructured audio masking.

2.1 Unimodal ASR Model

Our unimodal ASR model is a word-level (Palaskar and Metze, 2018) sequence-to-sequence model with attention (Bahdanau et al., 2016; Chan et al., 2016), identical to the model used in (Srinivasan et al., 2020). The encoder ($\mathbf{E}$) consists of 6 bidirectional LSTM layers (Schuster and Paliwal, 1997; Hochreiter and Schmidhuber, 1997) with temporal sub-sampling (Chan et al., 2016) in the middle two layers. The decoder is a two-layer conditional gated-recurrent-unit (Cho et al., 2014) which computes attention over the encoder states $\mathbf{E}$.

$$\mathbf{h}_t^{\mathbf{dec1}} = \mathrm{GRU}_1(\mathbf{y}_{t-1}, \mathbf{h}_{t-1}^{\mathbf{dec1}}) \qquad (1)$$

$$\mathbf{z}_t = \mathrm{Attention}(\mathbf{E}, \mathbf{h}_t^{\mathbf{dec1}}) \qquad (2)$$

$$\mathbf{h}_t^{\mathbf{dec2}} = \mathrm{GRU}_2(\mathbf{z}_t, \mathbf{h}_{t-1}^{\mathbf{dec2}}) \qquad (3)$$

---

[1]We note that RandWordMask is different from robust ASR (Barker et al., 2018) scenarios, where the whole signal is corrupted with stationary noise.

2.2 Multimodal ASR Models

We explore several fusion methods to integrate a visual feature vector $\mathbf{v}$ into the unimodal ASR model.

Encoder Feature Fusion: We use a visual adaptation method similar to (Caglayan et al., 2019), which we call **Shift Adaptation**. The visual feature vector $\mathbf{v}$ is projected down to the speech feature dimension; the resulting "shift vector" $\mathbf{s}$ is then added to the input speech features at all timesteps.

$$\mathbf{s} = \mathbf{W_v}\mathbf{f} + \mathbf{b} \qquad (4)$$
$$\mathbf{x_t} = \mathbf{x_t} + \mathbf{s} \qquad \forall \mathbf{t} \in \{1, ..., T\} \qquad (5)$$

Decoder Feature Fusion: Instead of integrating the visual features into the encoder, we can integrate them in the decoder. We hypothesize that this will bias the ASR's language modelling capacity. Anastasopoulos *et al.*(Anastasopoulos et al., 2019) explore several strategies for incorporating visual features into an LSTM language model. We employ similar fusion methods in our decoder.

1. **Early Decoder Fusion (Early-DF):** At each timestep, we concatenate $\mathbf{v}$ to the input embedding $\mathbf{y_t}$, which is then projected down to the embedding dimension.

$$\mathbf{y_t} = \mathbf{W_{proj}}[\mathbf{y_t}; \mathbf{v}] \qquad (6)$$

2. **Weighted Early Decoder Fusion (Weighted-DF):** We calculate a timestep-dependent weighted scalar between the input embedding $\mathbf{y_t}$ and the embedded visual features $\mathbf{v}$ (Eqn. 7), which scales the contribution of the visual features in the concatenated input (Eqn. 8):

$$\lambda = \sigma(\mathbf{y_t} \cdot \mathbf{v}) \qquad (7)$$
$$\mathbf{y_t} = \mathbf{W_{proj}}[\mathbf{y_t}; \lambda\mathbf{v}] \qquad (8)$$

3. **Middle Decoder Fusion (Middle-DF):** In this approach, fusion occurs between the GRU layers at $\mathbf{z_t}$ (Eqn. 2), which is the input to the 2nd decoder layer:

$$\mathbf{z_t} = \mathbf{W_{proj}}[\mathbf{z_t}; \mathbf{v}] \qquad (9)$$

4. **Hierarchical Attention over Features (HierAttn-DF):** In this approach, we add a hierarchical attention layer (Libovický and Helcl, 2017) that attends between the encoder context vector $\mathbf{z_t}$ (Eqn. 2) and the visual feature vector $\mathbf{v}$. The hierarchical context vector $\mathbf{z_t^{hier}}$ is the input to the second decoder layer (Eqn. 3):

$$\mathbf{z_t^{hier}} = \text{Attention}(\{\mathbf{z_t}, \mathbf{v}\}, \mathbf{h_t^{dec1}}) \qquad (10)$$

By conditioning the hierarchical attention on the output of the first decoder layer, the attention layer learns to decide which of the audio and visual modalities is more important for decoding at a given timestep.

2.3 Unstructured Masked Audio: RandWordMask

We simulate a degradation of the audio signal by randomly masking words in the audio with silence. This approach differs from (Srinivasan et al., 2020), where they masked a fixed set of words corresponding to entities, i.e., nouns and places. Figure 1 shows an example of an audio spectrogram with **RandWordMask**. The intuition behind random word masking, as opposed to entity-based word masking, is that noise in the audio signals is unlikely to systematically occur when someone is speaking about an entity. Our multimodal ASR models need to be responsive to audio that drops outside systematically expected regions.

In real-world settings, the rate at which the speech is masked (unavailable) is highly variable. Therefore, we train the models with an augmented version of the dataset: for each audio utterance, we create four masked audio samples, where words are masked with 0%, 20%, 40% and 60% probability. Note that the text transcript ($\mathbf{y_{1...N}}$) and image modality ($\mathbf{v}$) remain intact. This approach to augmenting the dataset will result in models that can adapt to different amounts of corruption in the audio signal during evaluation.

3 Experimental Setup

3.1 Dataset

We perform experiments on the Flickr 8K Audio Caption Corpus (Harwath and Glass, 2015), which contains 40,000 spoken captions (total 65 hours of speech) corresponding to 8,000 natural images from the Flickr8K dataset (Hodosh et al., 2015). The augmented dataset that we use for training and testing (as described in Section 2.3) consists of 160,000 spoken captions.

In addition, we use the SpeechCOCO dataset (Havard et al., 2017) for pretraining. SpeechCOCO contains over 600 hours of *synthesised* speech paired with images.

3.2 Implementation Details

3.2.1 Audio Features

We extract 43-dimensional filter bank features in an identical manner to (Srinivasan et al., 2020). In order to mask the audio, we first extract word-audio alignments from a pre-trained GMM-HMM model and expand the start and end timing marks by 25% of the segment duration to account for misalignments. We mask words in the audio by replacing word segments with 0.5 seconds silence.

3.2.2 Visual Features

We extract visual features from a ResNet-50 CNN (He et al., 2016) pre-trained on ImageNet. Specifically, we extract features from the 2048-dim average pooling layer, and project these to 256-dim through a learned linear layer: $\mathbf{v} = \mathbf{W} \cdot \text{CNN}(\mathbf{img})$

3.2.3 Model Implementation

We use the same model hyperparameters as in (Srinivasan et al., 2020). Models are trained using the *nmtpytorch* framework (Caglayan et al., 2017). We first pre-train our models for 25,000 minibatches on the SpeechCOCO dataset. This pre-training step, inspired by (Ilharco et al., 2019), was crucial to ensure stable training of our models on the Flickr 8K dataset.

3.3 Evaluation Metrics

Our model evaluation (Table 1a) has been conducted on the development set of Flickr8k-Audio, while the rest of our analysis is conducted on the test set. We report **WER** for all our models. For datasets where words have been masked in the audio signal, we compute **Recovery Rate** (Srinivasan et al., 2020), which measures the percentage of masked words which have been correctly recovered in the transcription.

In addition, we can determine the contribution of the visual signal when decoding each word in the HierAttn-DF model. We do this by inspecting the weights of the audio and visual modalities in the hierarchical attention mechanism. We introduce a new metric to quantify this: **Grounding Rate (G.R.)**.

$$\text{G.R.} = \frac{\#\text{recovered words where visual attn} > 0.5}{\#\text{correctly recovered masked words}}$$

We choose 0.5 as the threshold since above this value, more attention was given to the visual modality than the audio. G.R. thus represents the percentage of recovered words where the model was focusing more on the visual context while decoding.

4 Results and Analysis

In Table 1a, we summarize the performance of our unimodal ASR and proposed multimodal ASR models. Our development set is constructed similarly to our training set described in Section 2.3, consisting of samples with 0%, 20%, 40% and 60% of words masked. We examine performance on this Augmented dataset, as well as datasets at each individual masking level.

We see that the Decoder-Fusion (DF) multimodal models outperform unimodal ASR on both WER and RR. However, the best-performing models on both metrics differ: Weighted-DF achieves the lowest WER, with an improvement of 1.40% on the augmented dataset. HierAttn-DF has the best Recovery Rate, with an absolute improvement of 4% over the Unimodal model. These trends hold across all masking levels. Moreover, we observe that as the amount of masking in the audio signal increases, the WER and RR gains of our models increase. The ShiftAdapt model, which integrates the visual features with the speech encoder input, does not show any improvements over unimodal ASR. We observe that ShiftAdapt shows improvements when trained and tested on clean data, which aligns with the regularization signal previously observed in (Caglayan et al., 2019).

The results in Table 1a show that multimodality can recover words which were masked in an unstructured manner. We now turn our attention to analysing which types of words are recovered better. We conduct this analysis across seven categories: five syntactic (nouns, verbs, adjectives, adverbs and cardinals) and two semantic (places and colors).[2] For each category, we create a new test set where we mask all word occurrences. We note that these categories are varying degrees of "groundable", which we define as how easily identifiable they are in the visual modality - the more groundable a category, the easier it is to identify words belonging to that category in the visual context. Nouns and places are the most groundable categories, while adjectives and colors are also frequently easy to identify in the image. Verbs and adverbs, however, are less groundable categories.

In Table 1b, we compare the Recovery Rate of

---

[2] Words for the syntactic categories were found by POS tagging the dataset and keeping the top 100 frequent words.

Masking Perc.	↑ Recovery Rate (%)				↓ Word Error Rate (%)				
	Aug.	20%	40	60%	Aug.	0% (Clean)	20%	40%	60%
Unimodal	29.3	36.5	30.9	24.7	34.0	13.7	26.3	40.7	57.1
ShiftAdapt	29.3	36.5	31.3	25.1	34.0	13.5	25.9	40.5	57.1
Early-DF	32.0	38.2	33.2	28.7	33.3	13.7	25.9	39.7	55.3
Weighted-DF	33.0	38.8	34.5	29.6	**32.6**	**13.4**	**25.5**	**38.9**	**53.9**
Middle-DF	32.4	37.9	34.1	29.7	34.1	14.6	26.9	40.3	55.3
HierAttn-DF	**33.5**	**40.3**	**35.2**	**30.1**	33.2	13.9	25.9	39.3	54.7

(a) Recovery Rate (RR) and Word Error Rate (WER) of the ASR models on the FACC development set.

Metric	Model	Nouns	Places	Adj.	Colors	Verbs	Adverbs	Cardinals
RR (%)	Unimodal	37.2	28.0	26.0	26.6	26.0	30.4	56.7
	HierAttn-DF	47.9	40.0	29.7	30.4	27.9	29.2	58.1
Rel. Δ RR (%)	-	28.8	42.8	14.2	14.3	7.3	-3.9	2.4
G.R. (%)	HierAttn-DF	92.7	92.5	76.8	75.5	67.6	33.5	82.3

(b) Comparison of Recovery Rates of unimodal and HierAttn-DF ASR on various syntactic and semantic word categories.

Table 1: Recovery Rate, Word Error Rate, and Grounding Rates for the proposed models on the FACC dataset.

the unimodal ASR and HierAttn-DF (the best multimodal model in terms of RR) on the different word types. We observe that on the groundable entities *i.e.*, nouns and places, there is a relative improvement of at least 25% compared to the Unimodal model. Adjectives and colors, which are also groundable in the visual modality, are recovered around 14% better than the Unimodal model. The relative RR improvement for verbs is around 7%, whereas adverbs recovery is 4% worse. These results show that visual context can recover words from a variety of categories, even though it is better at recovering entities, and struggles with words that are less groundable in the image.

4.1 Hierarchical Attention Analysis

In Table 1b, we also summarize the Grounding Rate of HierAttn-DF when recovering different types of words. We find that the most groundable words (nouns and places), have a Grounding Rate > 90%. This means that 90% of the time the nouns/places were correctly recovered, the visual modality was being attended to. Adjectives and verbs, which are also groundable, have a grounding rate of ≈ 76%. These trends confirm that the model's improvements in masked word recovery are coming from using the visual signal.

In addition to calculating the Grounding Rate,

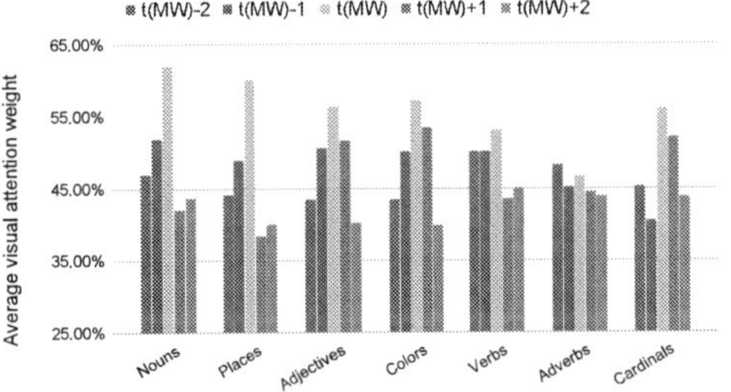

Figure 3: Average visual attention weight preceding and proceeding the onset of the masked word at timestep t(MW).

we also check whether the model learns to "look" at the visual modality when it encounters a masked word. In Figure 3, we plot the average visual attention weight at the masked word timestep, as well as the two preceding and proceeding timesteps. We see that the more groundable the word category, the more attention it learns to pay to the visual modality when the word is masked.

In Table 2, we present some qualitative examples where we visualize how the attention to each modality evolves with time. We observe that the timesteps corresponding to masked words in the signal have significantly higher visual attention. We see that in the first example, all masked words are correctly recovered. In the second example,

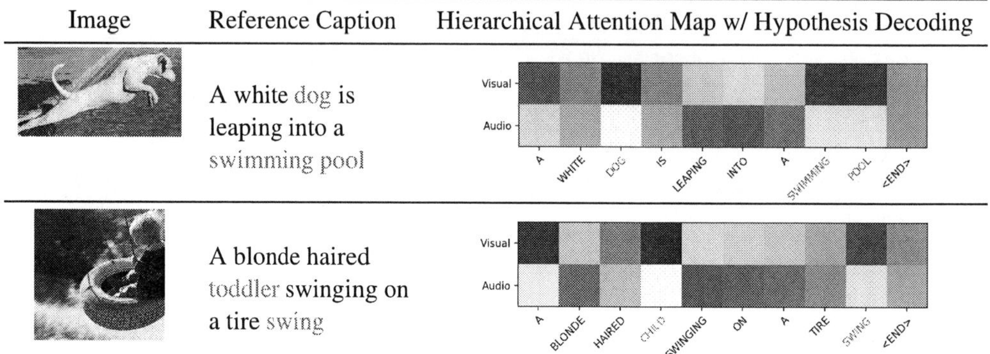

A white dog is leaping into a swimming pool

A blonde haired toddler swinging on a tire swing

Table 2: Examples of the HierAttn-DF model attending to the visual modality to recover masked words

however, the model replaces the word *toddler* with *child*, which are semantically similar and visually identical, showing that the model knows what to recover in the image but does not always recover it in the correct form.

4.2 Utility of RandWordMask Training

We compare our RandWordMask training scheme with the EntityMask training mechanism from (Srinivasan et al., 2020). In EntityMasking, only entities (nouns) are masked during training, and we hypothesize that this makes the model better at recovering entities but unable to generalize to other word types. Since RandWordMask training involves masking words at random, we expect the model should be able to generalize better to other words types. In Table 3, we compare the performance of the HierAttn-DF model when trained with three different training mechanisms: (i) None: no words are masked during training, (ii) EntityMask: top 100 frequent nouns are masked, (iii) RandWordMask. As expected, when trained without masking in the training set (None), the model recovers almost none of the masked words. While EntityMasking shows strong performance on recovering nouns and places (which are closely related), it doesn't

Masked Word	None	EntityMask	RandWordMask
Nouns	4.3	59.1	47.9
Places	2.4	43.1	40.0
Adjectives	0.7	4.7	29.7
Colors	1.3	3.4	30.3
Verbs	0.7	11.9	27.9
Adverbs	1.1	4.6	29.2
Cardinals	3.5	4.3	58.1

Table 3: RR (%) of different training schemes

Silence Masking		
Masking %	Unimodal	HierAttn-DF
20%	36.6	40.6
40%	31.1	36.0
60%	25.7	31.3
Whitenoise Masking		
Masking %	Unimodal	HierAttn-DF
20%	33.1	37.4
40%	26.7	32.1
60%	21.5	28.1

Table 4: RR (%) of unimodal and HierAttn-DF ASR models when trained and tested on silence and white noise masked audio, at different masking levels

generalize to the other syntactic/semantic word types. RandWordMask results in slightly worse performance on noun recovery, but it generalizes much better to other word categories.

4.3 Silence vs Whitenoise Masking

Our results in Tables 1a and 1b are performed in the experimental setting where words are masked with silence. However, another masking strategy explored in (Srinivasan et al., 2020) is white noise masking, where the masked word is replaced with white noise in the audio signal. (Srinivasan et al., 2020) had reported results in both masking scenarios, and noted that the improvements of the multimodal ASR model were similar in both scenarios. We further verify this by training unimodal and HierAttn-DF ASR models using RandWordMask, but with white noise masking instead of silence.

In Table 4, we report the Recovery Rates of both ASR models in both silence and white noise

Masking %	Congruent	Incongruent
20%	40.6	29.3
40%	36.0	24.7
60%	31.3	20.2

Table 5: Recovery Rates (%) for the HierAttn-DF model when provided with correct (congruent) and misaligned (incongruent) image

masking scenarios. We observe that while recovery is generally harder with white noise masking (evidenced by lower RR of both unimodal and multimodal ASR models), the HierAttn-DF model shows approximately the same absolute improvements in RR over the unimodal ASR. This indicates that the multimodal model can be applied to the more difficult white noise masking as well.

4.4 Congruency Analysis

We perform a sanity check of our model by misaligning audio utterances and images while decoding the trained model (Elliott, 2018). This evaluation quantifies the sensitivity of the model towards the visual modality. A model that is sensitive to the visual context would perform significantly worse when presented with an unrelated (*incongruent*) image during evaluation. Since the model has been trained to actively use the image, it is likely to extract incorrect information. In Table 5, we see that the HierAttn-DF model is substantially affected by the unrelated images (the recovery rate drops on average by 7%). This verifies that our multimodal models are sensitive to the image modality.

5   Conclusions

We show that visual signals improve multimodal speech recognition when the audio signal is subject to unstructured masking. RandWordMask simulates a wider range of noisy scenarios by masking different types of words in the audio signal during training and evaluation, as opposed to previous work that only masked groundable entities (Srinivasan et al., 2020). Future work involves developing new models that attend over visual features extracted from object proposals, which provide better visual signals.

Acknowledgments

This work used the computational resources of the PSC Bridges cluster at Extreme Science and Engineering Discovery Environment (XSEDE) (Towns et al., 2014)

References

Antonios Anastasopoulos, Shankar Kumar, and Hank Liao. 2019. Neural language modeling with visual features. *arXiv preprint arXiv:1903.02930*.

Stanislaw Antol, Aishwarya Agrawal, Jiasen Lu, Margaret Mitchell, Dhruv Batra, C Lawrence Zitnick, and Devi Parikh. 2015. VQA: Visual Question Answering. In *International Conference on Computer Vision (ICCV)*.

Dzmitry Bahdanau, Jan Chorowski, Dmitriy Serdyuk, Philemon Brakel, and Yoshua Bengio. 2016. End-to-end attention-based large vocabulary speech recognition. In *International Conference on Acoustics, Speech and Signal Processing (ICASSP)*.

Jon Barker, Shinji Watanabe, Emmanuel Vincent, and Jan Trmal. 2018. The fifth 'chime' speech separation and recognition challenge: Dataset, task and baselines. In *Interspeech*.

Ozan Caglayan, Mercedes García-Martínez, Adrien Bardet, Walid Aransa, Fethi Bougares, and Loïc Barrault. 2017. Nmtpy: A flexible toolkit for advanced neural machine translation systems. *Prague Bulletion of Math. Linguistics*.

Ozan Caglayan, Pranava Madhyastha, Lucia Specia, and Loïc Barrault. 2019. Probing the need for visual context multimodal machine translation. In *North American Chapter of the Association for Computational Linguistics (NAACL)*.

Ozan Caglayan, Ramon Sanabria, Shruti Palaskar, Loïc Barrault, and Florian Metze. 2019. Multimodal Grounding for Sequence-to-Sequence Speech Recognition. In *International Conference on Acoustics, Speech and Signal Processing (ICASSP)*.

William Chan, Navdeep Jaitly, Quoc Le, and Oriol Vinyals. 2016. Listen, attend and spell: A neural network for large vocabulary conversational speech recognition. In *International Conference on Acoustics, Speech and Signal Processing (ICASSP)*.

Kyunghyun Cho, Bart van Merriënboer, Caglar Gulcehre, Dzmitry Bahdanau, Fethi Bougares, Holger Schwenk, and Yoshua Bengio. 2014. Learning phrase representations using rnn encoder–decoder for statistical machine translation. In *Empirical Methods in Natural Language Processing (EMNLP)*.

Desmond Elliott. 2018. Adversarial evaluation of multimodal machine translation. In *Empirical Methods in Natural Language Processing (EMNLP)*.

Gabriel Grand and Yonatan Belinkov. 2019. Adversarial regularization for visual question answering: Strengths, shortcomings, and side effects. In *North American Chapter of the Association for Computational Linguistics (NAACL)*.

David Harwath and James Glass. 2015. Deep multimodal semantic embeddings for speech and images. In *Automatic Speech Recognition and Understanding (ASRU)*.

William Havard, Laurent Besacier, and Olivier Rosec. 2017. Speech-coco: 600k visually grounded spoken captions aligned to mscoco data set. In *International Workshop on Grounding Language Understanding (GLU)*.

Kaiming He, Xiangyu Zhang, Shaoqing Ren, and Jian Sun. 2016. Deep residual learning for image recognition. In *Computer Vision and Pattern Recognition (CVPR)*.

Sepp Hochreiter and Jürgen Schmidhuber. 1997. Long short-term memory. *Neural computation*.

Micah Hodosh, Peter Young, and Julia Hockenmaier. 2015. Framing image description as a ranking task: Data, models and evaluation metrics (extended abstract). In *International Joint Conference on Artificial Intelligence IJCAI*.

Gabriel Ilharco, Yuan Zhang, and Jason Baldridge. 2019. Large-scale representation learning from visually grounded untranscribed speech. In *Computational Natural Language Learning (CoNLL)*.

Jindřich Libovický and Jindřich Helcl. 2017. Attention strategies for multi-source sequence-to-sequence learning. In *Association for Computational Linguistics (ACL)*.

Shruti Palaskar, Jindřich Libovický, Spandana Gella, and Florian Metze. 2019. Multimodal abstractive summarization for how2 videos. In *Association for Computational Linguistics (ACL)*.

Shruti Palaskar and Florian Metze. 2018. Acoustic-to-word recognition with sequence-to-sequence models. In *Spoken Language Technology Workshop (SLT)*.

Shruti Palaskar, Ramon Sanabria, and Florian Metze. 2018. End-to-end multimodal speech recognition. In *International Conference on Acoustics, Speech and Signal Processing (ICASSP)*.

Sainandan Ramakrishnan, Aishwarya Agrawal, and Stefan Lee. 2018. Overcoming language priors in visual question answering with adversarial regularization. In *Advances in Neural Information Processing Systems (NeurIPS)*.

Ramon Sanabria, Ozan Caglayan, Shruti Palaskar, Desmond Elliott, Loïc Barrault, Lucia Specia, and Florian Metze. 2018. How2: a large-scale dataset for multimodal language understanding. In *Workshop on Visually Grounded Interaction and Language (ViGIL), NeurIPS*.

Mike Schuster and Kuldip K Paliwal. 1997. Bidirectional recurrent neural networks. *IEEE transactions on Signal Processing*.

Tejas Srinivasan, Ramon Sanabria, and Florian Metze. 2020. Looking enhances listening: Recovering missing speech using images. In *International Conference on Acoustics, Speech and Signal Processing (ICASSP)*.

Umut Sulubacak, Ozan Caglayan, Stig-Arne Grönroos, Aku Rouhe, Desmond Elliott, Lucia Specia, and Jörg Tiedemann. 2019. Multimodal machine translation through visuals and speech. *arXiv preprint arXiv:1911.12798*.

J. Towns, T. Cockerill, M. Dahan, I. Foster, K. Gaither, A. Grimshaw, V. Hazlewood, S. Lathrop, D. Lifka, G. D. Peterson, R. Roskies, J. Scott, and N. Wilkins-Diehr. 2014. Xsede: Accelerating scientific discovery. *Computing in Science and Engineering*, 16(05):62–74.

Building a Bridge: A Method for Image-Text Sarcasm Detection Without Pretraining on Image-Text Data

Xinyu Wang[1], Xiaowen Sun[1], Tan Yang[2], Hongbo Wang[1]
[1]State Key Laboratory of Networking and Switching Technology,
Beijing University of Posts and Telecommunications
[2]School of Computer Science (National Pilot Software Engineering School),
Beijing University of Posts and Telecommunications
[1,2]{xinyu.wang, sxw, tyang, hbwang}@bupt.edu.cn

Abstract

Sarcasm detection in social media with text and image is becoming more challenging. Previous works of image-text sarcasm detection were mainly to fuse the summaries of text and image: different sub-models read the text and image respectively to get the summaries, and fuses the summaries. Recently, some multi-modal models based on the architecture of BERT are proposed such as ViLBERT. However, they can only be pretrained on the image-text data. In this paper, we propose an image-text model for sarcasm detection using the pretrained BERT and ResNet without any further pretraining. BERT and ResNet have been pretrained on much larger text or image data than image-text data. We connect the vector spaces of BERT and ResNet to utilize more data. We use the pretrained Multi-Head Attention of BERT to model the text and image. Besides, we propose a 2D-Intra-Attention to extract the relationships between words and images. In experiments, our model outperforms the state-of-the-art model.

1 Introduction

It is becoming popular today for people using text with images to express their emotions and feelings in social media. This makes sarcasm detection more challenging. Sometimes, only when the text and image are read together can one know whether it is sarcasm. For example in Figure 1, which are from the multimodal Twitter dataset (Cai et al., 2019), the images contain the necessary information to determine whether it is a sarcasm.

The previous works about the image-text sarcasm detection (Cai et al., 2019) and also the image-text sentiment analysis (Gaspar and Alexandre, 2019; Huang et al., 2019; Zhao et al., 2019; Kruk et al., 2019) have about two steps: (1) summarizing the image and text; (2) fusing the summaries of the image and text. Although some works try to

explore the early fusion, it is still limited. Some details of text and image would be dropped when summarizing.

Recently, some multi-modal models based on the architecture of BERT are proposed such as ViL-BERT (Lu et al., 2019a,b), LXMERT (Tan and Bansal, 2019), VisualBERT (Li et al., 2019), and B2T2 (Alberti et al., 2019). However, these models are pretrained only on image-text data. In contrast, BERT can be pretrained on much lager text data than image-text data. ResNet can also make use of more image data.

In linear algebra, matrix multiplication can be understood as a kind of vector space transformation. In this paper, we provide a new perspective, the vector space transformation perspective, on this task. We propose a model to connect the text and image, and design a Bridge Layer to build the connection. The low-level and high-level image features are passed into BERT (Devlin et al., 2019) as the embedding of BERT.

We use the pretrained BERT and pretrained ResNet directly without any further pretraining for this task. Any BERT-like models that are based on Transformer (Vaswani et al., 2017) can still be used in our model in the future. Any visual models can be used in our model in the future as well. Besides, our model does not require huge computing resources and time for pretraining.

Based on the idea that sarcasm relies on the semantic relationships and contrasts between words, Tay et al. (2018) uses a softmax and a max function to extract the relationships and contrasts. However, the max function drops some information. In this paper, we propose a method called 2D-Intra-Attention with a 2D-softmax to handle the 2D relationships. Assuming n is the number of inputs, with the 2D-softmax, n^2 relationships are considered every time. In contrast, with the max function (Tay et al., 2018), only n relationships are con-

Proceedings of the First International Workshop on Natural Language Processing Beyond Text, pages 19–29
Online, November 20, 2020. ©2020 Association for Computational Linguistics
http://www.aclweb.org/anthology/W23-20%2d

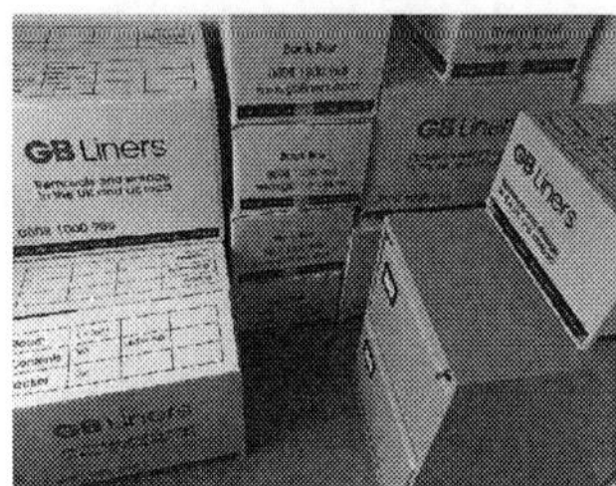

(a) "packing is so relaxing"

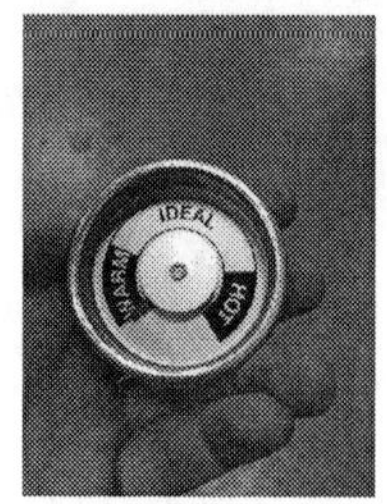

(b) "finally! a thermometer that meets my precision requirements for cooking."

Figure 1: Examples of image-text sarcasm.

sidered. Besides, we also add the image features into the 2D-Intra-Attention, so the relationships between words and images are considered.

In experiments, our model outperforms the state-of-the-art model. Our main contributions are summarized as follows:

- We connect the text and image: we use image features extracted by pretrained ResNet as the input of the pretrained BERT and utilize the Multi-Head Attention of BERT to model the image features.

- We propose a 2D-softmax to model the 2D relationships considering n^2 relationships and add image features to the 2D-Intra-Attention to extract the relationships and contrasts between words and images.

- We use the pretrained BERT and ResNet directly. Our model can adopt new BERT-like models or visual models in the future and does not require extra computing resources and time for pretraining.

2 Related Work

2.1 Text-Only Sarcasm Detection

Earlier works about sarcasm detection mainly focused on the text. Traditional methods consider and extract various features (Carvalho et al., 2009; Davidov et al., 2010; Veale and Hao, 2010; González-Ibáñez et al., 2011; Reyes et al., 2013; Riloff et al., 2013; Liebrecht et al., 2013; Ptáček et al., 2014; Barbieri et al., 2014; Rajadesingan et al., 2015; Bouazizi and Ohtsuki, 2015; Joshi et al., 2015), including n-grams, punctuations, sentiment, emoticons, incongruity, word frequency, syntactic patterns, etc. Then the deep learning came to sarcasm detection. Many methods based on CNN, LSTM (Hochreiter and Schmidhuber, 1997), and GRU (Cho et al., 2014) were proposed (Bamman and Smith, 2015; Ghosh and Veale, 2016; Zhang et al., 2016; Amir et al., 2016; Poria et al., 2016; Ghosh and Veale, 2017; Peled and Reichart, 2017; Felbo et al., 2017). The deep learning based methods achieved good performance. After the BERT was proposed (Devlin et al., 2019), some works tried to use BERT and achieve better performance (Castro et al., 2019; Badlani et al., 2019; Mao and Liu, 2019). However, these methods were mainly using the semantic features on the top layer extracted by BERT.

2.2 Multimodal Sarcasm Detection

Previous works explored the character and behavior of the reader for multimodal sarcasm detection (Mishra et al., 2016a,b). Some works tried to introduce visual information in sarcasm detection (Schifanella et al., 2016; Cai et al., 2019), but the fusion is mainly used for summaries. Besides sarcasm detection, some works about multimodal sentiment analysis have been done (Wang et al., 2017; Zadeh et al., 2017; Poria et al., 2015; Gu et al., 2018; Gaspar and Alexandre, 2019; Huang et al., 2019; Zhao et al., 2019). Some ideas of multimodal sentiment analysis are similar to multimodal sarcasm detection, so it is also possible to adapt our method to sentiment analysis in the future.

3 Approach

Figure 2 shows the architecture of our model. Our model contains two parts: Image-Text Fusion and 2D-Intra-Attention.

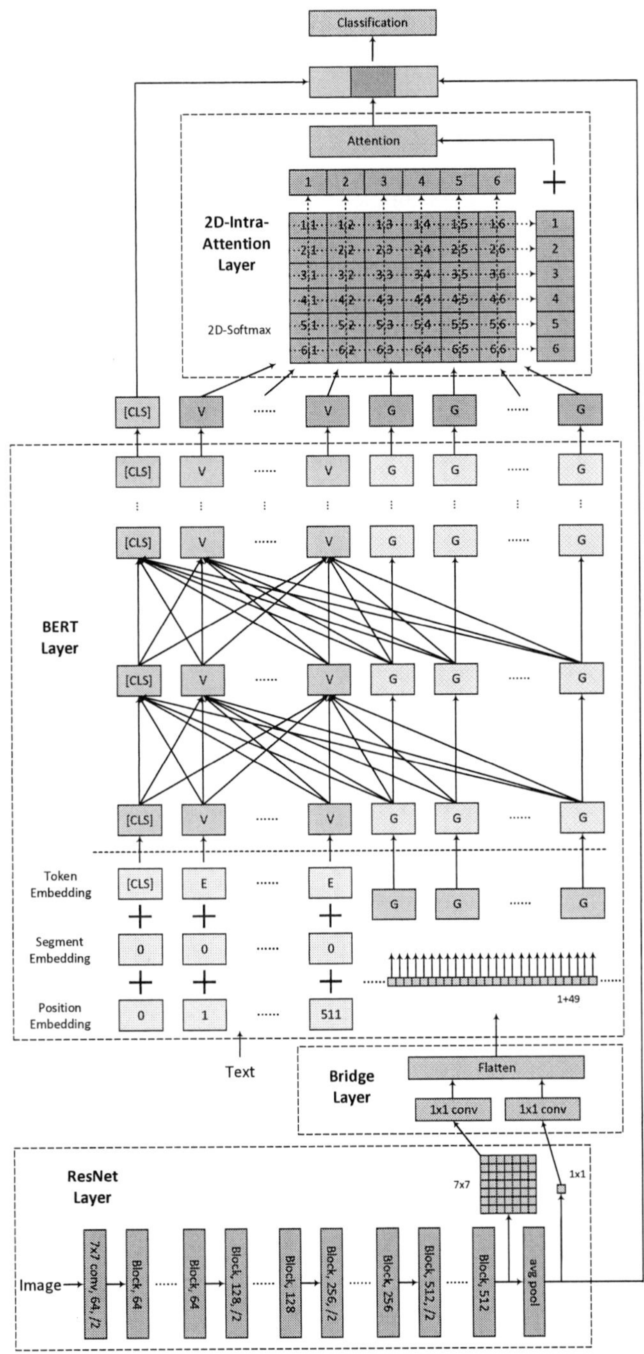

Figure 2: Architecture of our model, where "V" denotes the text and "G" denotes the image.

3.1 Image-Text Fusion

Image-Text Fusion includes BERT Layer, ResNet Layer, and Bridge Layer. In this paper, the term "BERT" refers to the BERT-like models (Devlin et al., 2019; Liu et al., 2019; Lan et al., 2019; Sanh et al., 2019), because any one of them and even the new BERT-like models in the future can be used in our model. Similarly, other visual models can also replace the ResNet (He et al., 2016) in our model.

3.1.1 ResNet Layer

ResNet Layer provides the detail and summary of an image. The "Block" of ResNet Layer in Figure 2 means the "building block" in (He et al., 2016), which contains two 3x3 convolution layers, or two 1x1 convolution layers and one 3x3 convolution layer. The image features are the tensor of size 7x7 after the "Block, 512" called feature 7x7 and the tensor of size 1x1 after "avg pool" called feature 1x1 in the following.

The feature 7x7 provides the details of the image. The feature 1x1 provides a summary of the image. In this way, every word in the text can pay attention to the different parts of the image and get more detail information.

3.1.2 Bridge Layer

Bridge Layer is to build the connection between ResNet and BERT. Bridge Layer is very important since ResNet and BERT are pretrained in different spaces. The image features of ResNet cannot be passed into BERT directly. The term "space" here means the vector space or semantic space and is to describe the representations of ResNet and BERT. Bridge Layer maps the image features from ResNet space into BERT space.

Formally, the image features of 7x7 and 1x1 are passed into two 1x1 convolutions respectively, one for feature 7x7 and another for feature 1x1. For the two 1x1 convolutions, the kernel size is 1x1, the stride is 1, the padding length is 0, the number of input channel is the number of the channel of image features such as 1024 or 2048, and the number of output channel is the hidden size of BERT such as 768 or 1024. The function of 1x1 convolutions here equals to fully connected layers. Using 1x1 convolutions and fully connected layers are both feasible when implementing the Bridge Layer. The outputs of the two 1x1 convolutions are flattened and passed into BERT as the embedding of BERT as shown in Figure 2.

The purpose of Bridge Layer is only to build the connection and do transformation instead of learning something. Other methods such as 3x3 conv are suboptimal because it is more likely to overfit than learning something we believe. The task of learning image information should be done by ResNet and the task of integrating image and text should be done by BERT.

3.1.3 BERT Layer

BERT Layer has two parts of inputs. One part is the normal text input. Another part is the image features that have been mapped into BERT space by Bridge Layer. The text is passed through the embedding layer and then the transformer, whereas the image features are passed into the transformer directly without going through the embedding layer.

The text and image features are passed through Multi-Head Attention in different ways. Formally, the attention for words of text is:

$$
\begin{aligned}
v_i^{(l)} =\text{MultiHeadAttention}(\\
v_1^{(l-1)}, v_2^{(l-1)}, \ldots, v_{|v|}^{(l-1)}, \\
g_1^{(l-1)}, g_2^{(l-1)}, \ldots, g_{|g|}^{(l-1)})
\end{aligned} \tag{1}
$$

where $v_i^{(l)}$ denotes the i-th word at the l-th layer and $g_i^{(l)}$ denotes the i-th image feature at the l-th layer; the $|v|$ denotes the number of words and the $|g|$ denotes the number of image features. In this way, every word v_i can pay attention to other words and image features. A word can get detail information from the 7x7 features and summary of the image from the 1x1 features.

However, the attention for image features is:

$$
g_i^{(l)} = \text{MultiHeadAttention}(g_i^{(l-1)}) \tag{2}
$$

Even though Bridge Layer has mapped image features into BERT space, the mapped image features are still not text, and BERT is never pretrained on the image features. Besides, the CNN of ResNet has a stronger capacity to learn images and the spatial relationships. The relationships between image features have been learned in ResNet. Image feature g_i can only "see" itself. The way of g_i passing through Multi-Head Attention is similar to passing through a fully connected layer. One head of the normal Multi-Head Attention (Vaswani et al., 2017) is:

$$
\text{Attention}(Q, K, V) = \text{softmax}(\frac{QK^T}{\sqrt{d_k}})V \tag{3}
$$

where Q, K, V are query, key, value. For the attention of g_i, the output of softmax will be 1 for g_i and be 0 for others. Therefore, the attention of one vector g_i of one head of the Multi-Head

Attention becomes:

$$\text{Attention}_g(\boldsymbol{Q_{g_i}}\boldsymbol{W}_Q, \boldsymbol{K}\boldsymbol{W}_K, \boldsymbol{V}\boldsymbol{W}_V)$$
$$= \text{softmax}\left(\frac{(\boldsymbol{Q_{g_i}}\boldsymbol{W}_Q)(\boldsymbol{K}\boldsymbol{W}_K)^T}{\sqrt{d_k}}\right)(\boldsymbol{V}\boldsymbol{W}_V)$$
$$= \boldsymbol{I_{g_i}}(\boldsymbol{V}\boldsymbol{W}_V) \qquad (4)$$
$$= (\boldsymbol{I_{g_i}}\boldsymbol{V})\boldsymbol{W}_V$$
$$= \boldsymbol{V_{g_i}}\boldsymbol{W}_V$$
$$= \boldsymbol{g}_i^T\boldsymbol{W}_V$$

$\boldsymbol{W}_Q \in \mathbb{R}^{m\times d}$, $\boldsymbol{W}_K \in \mathbb{R}^{m\times d}$, and $\boldsymbol{W}_V \in \mathbb{R}^{m\times d}$ are parameters for attention calculation as shown in (Vaswani et al., 2017); m denotes the hidden size of BERT and d denotes the hidden size of one head of Multi-Head Attention. $\boldsymbol{I_{g_i}} \in \mathbb{R}^{1\times n}$ is a vector where only the $(i + |\boldsymbol{v}|)$-th element is 1 and others are 0. n is the total number of words and image features, where $n = |\boldsymbol{v}| + |\boldsymbol{g}|$. $\boldsymbol{Q_{g_i}} \in \mathbb{R}^{1\times m}$ is the $(i + |\boldsymbol{v}|)$-th vector of $\boldsymbol{Q} \in \mathbb{R}^{n\times m}$. $\boldsymbol{V_{g_i}} \in \mathbb{R}^{1\times m}$ is the $(i + |\boldsymbol{v}|)$-th vector of $\boldsymbol{V} \in \mathbb{R}^{n\times m}$. The output of one head of attention of $\boldsymbol{g}_i \in \mathbb{R}^m$ is $\boldsymbol{g}_i^T\boldsymbol{W}_V$. The attention for $\boldsymbol{g}_i$ is only to map the $\boldsymbol{g}_i$ from the previous-layer semantic space into the next-layer semantic space with $\boldsymbol{W}_V$.

$\boldsymbol{g}_i$ "seeing" other words and images does not perform well because it will cause noises and overfitting. On the other hand, $\boldsymbol{g}_i$ has to "see" itself because the Multi-Head Attention layer can map the $\boldsymbol{g}_i$ from the previous layer into the next layer. If we use Bridge Layer to map the image features from image space into the next-layer semantic space directly, the model cannot utilize the existed parameters of BERT and need to learn the same information from the beginning.

3.1.4 Space Transformation

To explain the idea behind Image-Text Fusion that matrix multiplication is a kind of vector space transformation, Figure 3 shows the process in space view. Bridge Layer is the connection between the image space and the BERT embedding space. The image features are projected from image space into BERT embedding space by Bridge Layer. The Multi-Head Attention of BERT projects the image features from BERT embedding space into BERT Layer space, then projects the image features from the previous-layer space into next-layer space at every layer.

3.1.5 Some Details

In this section, we will introduce some important details about the Image-Text Fusion.

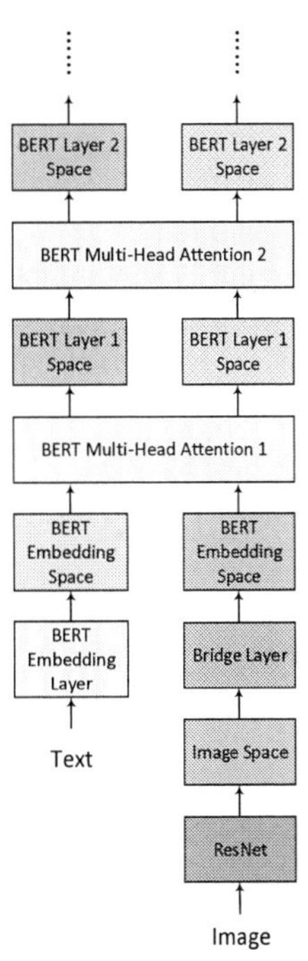

Figure 3: The space transformation view.

Learning Rate Since BERT and ResNet are pretrained models, they usually use a small learning rate. However, Bridge Layer is not pretrained and need to build the connection quickly. The learning rate of Bridge Layer should be greater than BERT and ResNet. In this way, Bridge Layer can learn fast and catch up with BERT and ResNet. This is very important because using the same learning rate will hinder the model from convergence. Empirically, we suggest that the learning rate of Bridge Layer should be at least 10x greater than BERT and ResNet.

Length Limitation The input length of BERT should be less than 512 because only 512 position embeddings are pretrained. However, the image features skip the embedding layer, so introducing image features will not influence the input length limitation of text.

Image Features Sequence The Multi-Head Attention does not consider position by itself, so BERT introduces the position embedding. However, since image features skip the position embedding, the input order of image features is trivial.

3.2 2D-Intra-Attention

We propose a 2D-softmax function to handle the 2D scores. We also add image features to the 2D-Intra-Attention to explore the contrasts and disparities between words and images.

Formally, we define the outputs of both words and images of BERT as $\{h_i\}_{i=1}^n$, where n is the total number of words and image features. In other words: $n = |v| + |g|, h_i = v_i, h_{i+|v|} = g_i$.

A pair is defined as:

$$h_{ij} = [h_i; h_j] \tag{5}$$

where $[.;.]$ denotes the concatenation and h_{ij} is a vector. Every h_{ij} is passed through a fully connected layer to get score s_{ij} as:

$$s_{ij} = W_s h_{ij} + b_s \tag{6}$$

where $W_s \in \mathbb{R}^{1 \times 2m}$ and $b_s \in \mathbb{R}^1$ are learnable parameters, and m denotes the hidden size of BERT. Then values of s_{ij} where $i = j$ are masked, which is similar to (Tay et al., 2018), and s_{ij} where $i > |v|$ and $j > |v|$ are masked as well.

The 2D-softmax is:

$$a_{ij} = \frac{e^{s_{ij}}}{\sum_{p=1}^{n} \sum_{q=1}^{n} e^{s_{pq}}} \tag{7}$$

This 2D-softmax considers s_{ij} from two dimension instead of only one. Then the attention weight $\hat{a}_i$ is calculated as:

$$\hat{a}_i = \frac{1}{2} \sum_{p=1}^{n} a_{ip} + \frac{1}{2} \sum_{q=1}^{n} a_{qi} \tag{8}$$

The a_{ij} in 2D is projected into the $\hat{a}_i$ in 1D. The a_{ip} and a_{qi} are divided by 2 because every a_{ij} is added twice. The final step of 2D-Intra-Attention is:

$$\hat{h} = \sum_i \hat{a}_i (W_a h_i) \tag{9}$$

where $W_a \in \mathbb{R}^{m \times m}$ is a learnable parameter.

With the 2D-softmax, n^2 pairs can be considered. For example, if a word has obvious contrasts with many other words or other parts of images, the attention weight of the word will be high.

3.3 Final Fusion

The concatenation of the [CLS] of BERT, the $\hat{h}$ from 2D-Intra-Attention, and the features 1x1 from ResNet are passed through a fully connected layer and a sigmoid function for classification.

4 Experiments

4.1 Training Details

In this section, we will introduce the details and hyper-parameters for training our model.

Pretrained model Pretrained BERT-base-uncased (Devlin et al., 2019) and RoBERTa-base (Liu et al., 2019) with 12 layers, and pretrained ResNet50 (He et al., 2016) with 50 layers are used. The ResNet50 we employ is provided by PyTorch (Paszke et al., 2019).

Optimizer The optimizer is Adam (Kingma and Ba, 2014) for BERT with linear schedule and a warm-up ratio of 0.05.

Learning rate The learning rate for RoBERTa and ResNet50 is 1e-5, and for other parameters including Bridge Layer is 1e-3.

Image preprocessing For predicting, we resize the original image making the smaller edge of the image is 224, then crop the image at the center. For training, we implement data augment for images including random crop and randomly change the brightness, contrast and saturation of the image.

Parameters number The number of parameters of our model for experiments is 151M. The learnable parameters are initialized by (He et al., 2015).

GPU & Environment The model is running on a GPU of NVIDIA GeForce RTX 2080 Ti. Due to the limited GPU RAM, we use gradient accumulation for training. The operating system is Ubuntu 18.04. We use PyTorch 1.4.0 (Paszke et al., 2019) and Transformers 2.4.1 (Wolf et al., 2019) to implement our model. We also use mixed precision training with NVIDIA Apex 0.1 (Micikevicius et al., 2017) to accelerate our model.

Running time It takes an average of 343 seconds per epoch. We run the model 10 times and record the best result.

Metrics The metrics for evaluation are F1-score, precision, recall, and accuracy, which are implemented by Scikit-learn (Pedregosa et al., 2011).

4.2 Comparison

The dataset for experiments is the multimodal image-text Twitter dataset (Cai et al., 2019). This data contains image and text as shown in Figure 1.

The description of other compared models are as follows:

	F1-score	Precision	Recall	Accuracy
IARN (Tay et al., 2018)	0.7894	0.7991	0.7799	0.8343
DMAF (Huang et al., 2019)	0.7891	0.7479	0.8352	0.8224
MMHFM (Cai et al., 2019)	0.8018	0.7657	0.8415	0.8344
VisualBERT (Li et al., 2019)	0.7968	0.7666	0.8294	0.8351
LXMERT (Tan and Bansal, 2019)	0.8014	0.7783	0.8259	0.8393
ViLBERT (Lu et al., 2019b)	0.8171	0.7752	0.8637	0.8468
Our model using BERT	0.8235	0.8001	0.8484	0.8564
Our model using RoBERTa	0.8605	0.8295	0.8939	0.8851

Table 1: Comparison of different models.

IARN Multi-dimensional Intra-Attention Recurrent Network (IARN) (Tay et al., 2018). This model proposed a looking in-between method for text-only sarcasm detection.

DMAF Deep Multimodal Attentive Fusion (DMAF) (Huang et al., 2019). We use this image-text sentiment analysis model in comparison since sarcasm detection and sentiment analysis share some similarities.

MMHFM Multi-Modal Hierarchical Fusion Model (MMHFM) (Cai et al., 2019), a fusion model for image-text sarcasm detection.

VisualBERT VisualBERT (Li et al., 2019) is a pretrained visual-text model for vision-and-language tasks, which consists of a stack of Transformer layers.

LXMERT LXMERT (Tan and Bansal, 2019) is a pretrained visual-text model learning the vision-and-language connections based on a large-scale Transformer model.

ViLBERT ViLBERT (Lu et al., 2019a,b) is a pretrained visual-text model which extends the BERT architecture to a multi-modal model. ViLBERT was proposed in (Lu et al., 2019a) at first, then was improved by multi-task training in (Lu et al., 2019b).

Table 1 shows the results. Since ViLBERT is based on BERT (Devlin et al., 2019), we also use BERT (Devlin et al., 2019) in our model to give a fair comparison. Our model with BERT outperforming other models verifies the effectiveness of our model. Moreover, due to the advantage that our model can adopt different pretrained models, if we use RoBERTa (Liu et al., 2019), which was proposed at the time close to ViLBERT, our model

can outperform other models significantly. One improvement of RoBERTa comes from using larger data, and our model can make use of the data by adopting RoBERTa.

Our model outperforming ViLBERT and other pretrained visual-text models is mainly because ViLBERT is only pretrained on limited image-text data. In contrast, our model utilizes more unsupervised text data and image data, and only needs to learn a transformation.

4.3 Ablation Studies

In this section, pretrained BERT-base-uncased (Devlin et al., 2019) and pretrained ResNet50 (He et al., 2016) are used. The term "classification" here means the classification layer at the top of Figure 2, which contains a fully connected layer and a sigmoid function. The description of different sets are as follows:

BERT A text-only model that uses the [CLS] of BERT (Devlin et al., 2019) for classification.

BERT + 1D-Intra-Att A text-only model that uses the output of 1D-Intra-Attention (Tay et al., 2018), whose inputs are the outputs of BERT, for classification.

BERT + 2D-Intra-Att A text-only model that uses the output of 2D-Intra-Attention, whose inputs are the outputs of BERT, for classification. 1D-Intra-Attention (Tay et al., 2018) was designed for text-only model, so we also add 2D-Intra-Attention to this text-only model to compare these two attentions.

Concatenation of BERT and ResNet An image-text model that concatenates the [CLS] of BERT whose inputs are text and the output of ResNet for classification. In other words, the model

	F1-score	Precision	Recall	Accuracy
BERT	0.8051	0.7741	0.8388	0.8381
BERT + 1D-Intra-Att	0.8074	0.7766	0.8407	0.8430
BERT + 2D-Intra-Att	0.8088	0.7782	0.8420	0.8439
Concatenation of BERT and ResNet	0.8144	0.7830	0.8485	0.8436
Concatenation of BERT and ResNet + 2D-Intra-Att	0.8168	0.7856	0.8505	0.8476
Image-Text Fusion	0.8214	0.7992	0.8449	0.8541
Image-Text Fusion with Bridge Layer using 3x3 conv	0.8202	0.7978	0.8438	0.8509
Image-Text Fusion + 2D-Intra-Att (our model)	0.8235	0.8001	0.8484	0.8564

Table 2: Ablation Studies.

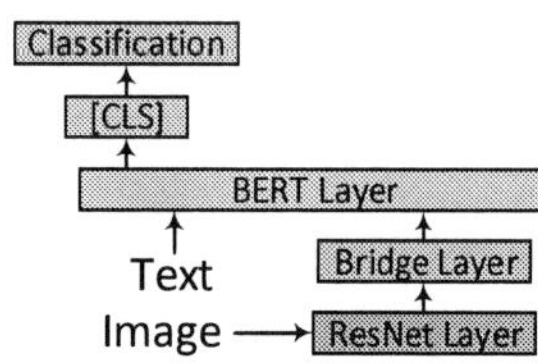

Figure 4: Overview of **Image-Text Fusion** used in ablation studies.

uses image features but does not use them as the inputs for BERT.

Concatenation of BERT and ResNet + 2D-Intra-Att   An image-text model that concatenates the [CLS] of BERT whose inputs are text, the output of ResNet, and the output of 2D-Intra-Attention for classification.

Image-Text Fusion   The Image-Text Fusion part in this paper. It is important to note that the output of ResNet is used in Final Fusion for classification instead of in Image-Text Fusion. We do not use the output of ResNet for classification here but only the [CLS] as shown in Figure 4, so the image information must go through Bridge Layer and BERT Layer to reach the classification. If Bridge Layer cannot transform image features or BERT Layer cannot integrate text and image, the result should be similar to **BERT** or even worse because image features may cause noises.

Image-Text Fusion with Bridge Layer using 3x3 conv   The Image-Text Fusion in this paper that uses the [CLS] of BERT for classification with Bridge Layer using 3x3 conv with padding length 1 instead of 1x1 conv.

Table 2 shows the results. Both **Image-Text Fusion** and **BERT** only use the [CLS] of BERT for classification, and the difference is that BERT Layer of **Image-Text Fusion** has image input. This is proof that BERT Layer and Bridge Layer are effective because image information must go through them to reach the classification. BERT Layer and Bridge Layer must handle image inputs well to give a better result. With image input, the score of **Concatenation of BERT and ResNet** is improved by 0.93% compared with **BERT**, but is still worse than ViLBERT. **Image-Text Fusion** achieves 1.63% improvement compared with **BERT** and outperforms ViLBERT without 2D-Intra-Attention.

The bad result of **Image-Text Fusion with Bridge Layer using 3x3 conv** verifies the effectiveness of using 1x1 conv in Bridge Layer. Our idea for Bridge Layer is just transforming so that the model can utilize pretrained parameters as much as possible instead of learning them from the beginning.

2D-Intra-Attention gives 0.14% improvement for **BERT + 2D-Intra-Att** compared with **BERT + 1D-Intra-Att** and 0.37% improvement compared with **BERT**. Also, 2D-Intra-Attention gives 0.21% improvement for **Image-Text Fusion + 2D-Intra-Att** compared with **Image-Text Fusion**.

5   Conclusion

In this paper, we propose an image-text model for image-text sarcasm detection. We propose a novel way to integrate image and text information. Our model outperforms the state-of-the-art model. Comparing with multi-modal models, our model utilizes more text and image data instead of only the image-text data. Our model can adopt different pretrained language models and visual models directly without any further pretraining.

26

References

Chris Alberti, Jeffrey Ling, Michael Collins, and David Reitter. 2019. Fusion of detected objects in text for visual question answering. In *Proceedings of the 2019 Conference on Empirical Methods in Natural Language Processing and the 9th International Joint Conference on Natural Language Processing (EMNLP-IJCNLP)*, pages 2131–2140, Hong Kong, China. Association for Computational Linguistics.

Silvio Amir, Byron C. Wallace, Hao Lyu, Paula Carvalho, and Mário J. Silva. 2016. Modelling context with user embeddings for sarcasm detection in social media. In *Proceedings of The 20th SIGNLL Conference on Computational Natural Language Learning*, pages 167–177, Berlin, Germany. Association for Computational Linguistics.

Rohan Badlani, Nishit Asnani, and Manan Rai. 2019. An ensemble of humour, sarcasm, and hate speech for sentiment classification in online reviews. In *Proceedings of the 5th Workshop on Noisy User-generated Text (W-NUT 2019)*, pages 337–345, Hong Kong, China. Association for Computational Linguistics.

David Bamman and Noah A Smith. 2015. Contextualized sarcasm detection on twitter. In *Ninth International AAAI Conference on Web and Social Media*.

Francesco Barbieri, Horacio Saggion, and Francesco Ronzano. 2014. Modelling sarcasm in twitter, a novel approach. In *Proceedings of the 5th Workshop on Computational Approaches to Subjectivity, Sentiment and Social Media Analysis*, pages 50–58, Baltimore, Maryland. Association for Computational Linguistics.

Mondher Bouazizi and Tomoaki Ohtsuki. 2015. Sarcasm detection in twitter:" all your products are incredibly amazing!!!"-are they really? In *2015 IEEE Global Communications Conference (GLOBECOM)*, pages 1–6. IEEE.

Yitao Cai, Huiyu Cai, and Xiaojun Wan. 2019. Multimodal sarcasm detection in twitter with hierarchical fusion model. In *Proceedings of the 57th Annual Meeting of the Association for Computational Linguistics*, pages 2506–2515, Florence, Italy. Association for Computational Linguistics.

Paula Carvalho, Luís Sarmento, Mário J Silva, and Eugénio De Oliveira. 2009. Clues for detecting irony in user-generated contents: oh...!! it's" so easy";-. In *Proceedings of the 1st international CIKM workshop on Topic-sentiment analysis for mass opinion*, pages 53–56.

Santiago Castro, Devamanyu Hazarika, Verónica Pérez-Rosas, Roger Zimmermann, Rada Mihalcea, and Soujanya Poria. 2019. Towards multimodal sarcasm detection (an _Obviously_ perfect paper). In *Proceedings of the 57th Annual Meeting of the Association for Computational Linguistics*, pages 4619–4629, Florence, Italy. Association for Computational Linguistics.

Kyunghyun Cho, Bart van Merriënboer, Caglar Gulcehre, Dzmitry Bahdanau, Fethi Bougares, Holger Schwenk, and Yoshua Bengio. 2014. Learning phrase representations using RNN encoder–decoder for statistical machine translation. In *Proceedings of the 2014 Conference on Empirical Methods in Natural Language Processing (EMNLP)*, pages 1724–1734, Doha, Qatar. Association for Computational Linguistics.

Dmitry Davidov, Oren Tsur, and Ari Rappoport. 2010. Semi-supervised recognition of sarcastic sentences in twitter and amazon. In *Proceedings of the Fourteenth Conference on Computational Natural Language Learning*, pages 107–116. Association for Computational Linguistics.

Jacob Devlin, Ming-Wei Chang, Kenton Lee, and Kristina Toutanova. 2019. BERT: Pre-training of deep bidirectional transformers for language understanding. In *Proceedings of the 2019 Conference of the North American Chapter of the Association for Computational Linguistics: Human Language Technologies, Volume 1 (Long and Short Papers)*, pages 4171–4186, Minneapolis, Minnesota. Association for Computational Linguistics.

Bjarke Felbo, Alan Mislove, Anders Søgaard, Iyad Rahwan, and Sune Lehmann. 2017. Using millions of emoji occurrences to learn any-domain representations for detecting sentiment, emotion and sarcasm. *arXiv preprint arXiv:1708.00524*.

António Gaspar and Luís A. Alexandre. 2019. A multimodal approach to image sentiment analysis. In *Intelligent Data Engineering and Automated Learning – IDEAL 2019*, pages 302–309, Cham. Springer International Publishing.

Aniruddha Ghosh and Tony Veale. 2016. Fracking sarcasm using neural network. In *Proceedings of the 7th Workshop on Computational Approaches to Subjectivity, Sentiment and Social Media Analysis*, pages 161–169, San Diego, California. Association for Computational Linguistics.

Aniruddha Ghosh and Tony Veale. 2017. Magnets for sarcasm: Making sarcasm detection timely, contextual and very personal. In *Proceedings of the 2017 Conference on Empirical Methods in Natural Language Processing*, pages 482–491, Copenhagen, Denmark. Association for Computational Linguistics.

Roberto González-Ibáñez, Smaranda Muresan, and Nina Wacholder. 2011. Identifying sarcasm in twitter: A closer look. In *Proceedings of the 49th Annual Meeting of the Association for Computational Linguistics: Human Language Technologies*, pages 581–586, Portland, Oregon, USA. Association for Computational Linguistics.

Yue Gu, Kangning Yang, Shiyu Fu, Shuhong Chen, Xinyu Li, and Ivan Marsic. 2018. Multimodal affective analysis using hierarchical attention strategy with word-level alignment. In *Proceedings of the 56th Annual Meeting of the Association for Computational Linguistics (Volume 1: Long Papers)*, pages 2225–2235, Melbourne, Australia. Association for Computational Linguistics.

Kaiming He, Xiangyu Zhang, Shaoqing Ren, and Jian Sun. 2015. Delving deep into rectifiers: Surpassing human-level performance on imagenet classification. In *The IEEE International Conference on Computer Vision (ICCV)*.

Kaiming He, Xiangyu Zhang, Shaoqing Ren, and Jian Sun. 2016. Deep residual learning for image recognition. In *The IEEE Conference on Computer Vision and Pattern Recognition (CVPR)*.

Sepp Hochreiter and Jürgen Schmidhuber. 1997. Long short-term memory. *Neural Computation*, 9(8):1735–1780.

Feiran Huang, Xiaoming Zhang, Zhonghua Zhao, Jie Xu, and Zhoujun Li. 2019. Image–text sentiment analysis via deep multimodal attentive fusion. *Knowledge-Based Systems*, 167:26–37.

Aditya Joshi, Vinita Sharma, and Pushpak Bhattacharyya. 2015. Harnessing context incongruity for sarcasm detection. In *Proceedings of the 53rd Annual Meeting of the Association for Computational Linguistics and the 7th International Joint Conference on Natural Language Processing (Volume 2: Short Papers)*, pages 757–762, Beijing, China. Association for Computational Linguistics.

Diederik P Kingma and Jimmy Ba. 2014. Adam: A method for stochastic optimization. *arXiv preprint arXiv:1412.6980*.

Julia Kruk, Jonah Lubin, Karan Sikka, Xiao Lin, Dan Jurafsky, and Ajay Divakaran. 2019. Integrating text and image: Determining multimodal document intent in instagram posts. *arXiv preprint arXiv:1904.09073*.

Zhenzhong Lan, Mingda Chen, Sebastian Goodman, Kevin Gimpel, Piyush Sharma, and Radu Soricut. 2019. Albert: A lite bert for self-supervised learning of language representations. *arXiv preprint arXiv:1909.11942*.

Liunian Harold Li, Mark Yatskar, Da Yin, Cho-Jui Hsieh, and Kai-Wei Chang. 2019. Visualbert: A simple and performant baseline for vision and language. *arXiv preprint arXiv:1908.03557*.

CC Liebrecht, FA Kunneman, and APJ van Den Bosch. 2013. The perfect solution for detecting sarcasm in tweets# not.

Yinhan Liu, Myle Ott, Naman Goyal, Jingfei Du, Mandar Joshi, Danqi Chen, Omer Levy, Mike Lewis, Luke Zettlemoyer, and Veselin Stoyanov. 2019. Roberta: A robustly optimized bert pretraining approach. *arXiv preprint arXiv:1907.11692*.

Jiasen Lu, Dhruv Batra, Devi Parikh, and Stefan Lee. 2019a. Vilbert: Pretraining task-agnostic visiolinguistic representations for vision-and-language tasks. In *Advances in Neural Information Processing Systems*, pages 13–23.

Jiasen Lu, Vedanuj Goswami, Marcus Rohrbach, Devi Parikh, and Stefan Lee. 2019b. 12-in-1: Multi-task vision and language representation learning. *arXiv preprint arXiv:1912.02315*.

Jihang Mao and Wanli Liu. 2019. A bert-based approach for automatic humor detection and scoring. In *Proceedings of the Iberian Languages Evaluation Forum (IberLEF 2019). CEUR Workshop Proceedings, CEUR-WS, Bilbao, Spain (9 2019)*.

Paulius Micikevicius, Sharan Narang, Jonah Alben, Gregory Diamos, Erich Elsen, David Garcia, Boris Ginsburg, Michael Houston, Oleksii Kuchaiev, Ganesh Venkatesh, et al. 2017. Mixed precision training. *arXiv preprint arXiv:1710.03740*.

Abhijit Mishra, Diptesh Kanojia, and Pushpak Bhattacharyya. 2016a. Predicting readers' sarcasm understandability by modeling gaze behavior. In *Thirtieth AAAI Conference on Artificial Intelligence*.

Abhijit Mishra, Diptesh Kanojia, Seema Nagar, Kuntal Dey, and Pushpak Bhattacharyya. 2016b. Harnessing cognitive features for sarcasm detection. In *Proceedings of the 54th Annual Meeting of the Association for Computational Linguistics (Volume 1: Long Papers)*, pages 1095–1104, Berlin, Germany. Association for Computational Linguistics.

Adam Paszke, Sam Gross, Francisco Massa, Adam Lerer, James Bradbury, Gregory Chanan, Trevor Killeen, Zeming Lin, Natalia Gimelshein, Luca Antiga, et al. 2019. Pytorch: An imperative style, high-performance deep learning library. In *Advances in Neural Information Processing Systems 32*, pages 8024–8035. Curran Associates, Inc.

F. Pedregosa, G. Varoquaux, A. Gramfort, V. Michel, B. Thirion, O. Grisel, M. Blondel, P. Prettenhofer, R. Weiss, V. Dubourg, J. Vanderplas, A. Passos, D. Cournapeau, M. Brucher, M. Perrot, and E. Duchesnay. 2011. Scikit-learn: Machine learning in Python. *Journal of Machine Learning Research*, 12:2825–2830.

Lotem Peled and Roi Reichart. 2017. Sarcasm SIGN: Interpreting sarcasm with sentiment based monolingual machine translation. In *Proceedings of the 55th Annual Meeting of the Association for Computational Linguistics (Volume 1: Long Papers)*, pages 1690–1700, Vancouver, Canada. Association for Computational Linguistics.

Soujanya Poria, Erik Cambria, and Alexander Gelbukh. 2015. Deep convolutional neural network textual features and multiple kernel learning for utterance-level multimodal sentiment analysis. In *Proceedings of the 2015 Conference on Empirical Meth-*

ods in *Natural Language Processing*, pages 2539–2544, Lisbon, Portugal. Association for Computational Linguistics.

Soujanya Poria, Erik Cambria, Devamanyu Hazarika, and Prateek Vij. 2016. A deeper look into sarcastic tweets using deep convolutional neural networks. In *Proceedings of COLING 2016, the 26th International Conference on Computational Linguistics: Technical Papers*, pages 1601–1612, Osaka, Japan. The COLING 2016 Organizing Committee.

Tomáš Ptáček, Ivan Habernal, and Jun Hong. 2014. Sarcasm detection on Czech and English twitter. In *Proceedings of COLING 2014, the 25th International Conference on Computational Linguistics: Technical Papers*, pages 213–223, Dublin, Ireland. Dublin City University and Association for Computational Linguistics.

Ashwin Rajadesingan, Reza Zafarani, and Huan Liu. 2015. Sarcasm detection on twitter: A behavioral modeling approach. In *Proceedings of the Eighth ACM International Conference on Web Search and Data Mining*, pages 97–106.

Antonio Reyes, Paolo Rosso, and Tony Veale. 2013. A multidimensional approach for detecting irony in twitter. *Language Resources and Evaluation*, 47(1):239–268.

Ellen Riloff, Ashequl Qadir, Prafulla Surve, Lalindra De Silva, Nathan Gilbert, and Ruihong Huang. 2013. Sarcasm as contrast between a positive sentiment and negative situation. In *Proceedings of the 2013 Conference on Empirical Methods in Natural Language Processing*, pages 704–714, Seattle, Washington, USA. Association for Computational Linguistics.

Victor Sanh, Lysandre Debut, Julien Chaumond, and Thomas Wolf. 2019. Distilbert, a distilled version of bert: Smaller, faster, cheaper and lighter. *arXiv preprint arXiv:1910.01108*.

Rossano Schifanella, Paloma de Juan, Joel Tetreault, and Liangliang Cao. 2016. Detecting sarcasm in multimodal social platforms. In *Proceedings of the 24th ACM International Conference on Multimedia*, pages 1136–1145.

Hao Tan and Mohit Bansal. 2019. LXMERT: Learning cross-modality encoder representations from transformers. In *Proceedings of the 2019 Conference on Empirical Methods in Natural Language Processing and the 9th International Joint Conference on Natural Language Processing (EMNLP-IJCNLP)*, pages 5100–5111, Hong Kong, China. Association for Computational Linguistics.

Yi Tay, Anh Tuan Luu, Siu Cheung Hui, and Jian Su. 2018. Reasoning with sarcasm by reading in-between. In *Proceedings of the 56th Annual Meeting of the Association for Computational Linguistics*

(Volume 1: Long Papers), pages 1010–1020, Melbourne, Australia. Association for Computational Linguistics.

Ashish Vaswani, Noam Shazeer, Niki Parmar, Jakob Uszkoreit, Llion Jones, Aidan N Gomez, Ł ukasz Kaiser, and Illia Polosukhin. 2017. Attention is all you need. In I. Guyon, U. V. Luxburg, S. Bengio, H. Wallach, R. Fergus, S. Vishwanathan, and R. Garnett, editors, *Advances in Neural Information Processing Systems 30*, pages 5998–6008. Curran Associates, Inc.

Tony Veale and Yanfen Hao. 2010. Detecting ironic intent in creative comparisons. In *ECAI*, volume 215, pages 765–770.

H. Wang, A. Meghawat, L. Morency, and E. P. Xing. 2017. Select-additive learning: Improving generalization in multimodal sentiment analysis. In *2017 IEEE International Conference on Multimedia and Expo (ICME)*, pages 949–954.

Thomas Wolf, Lysandre Debut, Victor Sanh, Julien Chaumond, Clement Delangue, Anthony Moi, Pierric Cistac, Tim Rault, R'emi Louf, Morgan Funtowicz, and Jamie Brew. 2019. Huggingface's transformers: State-of-the-art natural language processing. *ArXiv*, abs/1910.03771.

Amir Zadeh, Minghai Chen, Soujanya Poria, Erik Cambria, and Louis-Philippe Morency. 2017. Tensor fusion network for multimodal sentiment analysis. *arXiv preprint arXiv:1707.07250*.

Meishan Zhang, Yue Zhang, and Guohong Fu. 2016. Tweet sarcasm detection using deep neural network. In *Proceedings of COLING 2016, the 26th International Conference on Computational Linguistics: Technical Papers*, pages 2449–2460, Osaka, Japan. The COLING 2016 Organizing Committee.

Ziyuan Zhao, Huiying Zhu, Zehao Xue, Zhao Liu, Jing Tian, Matthew Chin Heng Chua, and Maofu Liu. 2019. An image-text consistency driven multimodal sentiment analysis approach for social media. *Information Processing & Management*, 56(6):102097.

A Benchmark for Structured Procedural Knowledge Extraction
from Cooking Videos

Frank F. Xu[1]*   Lei Ji[2]   Botian Shi[2]   Junyi Du[3]

Graham Neubig[1]   Yonatan Bisk[1]   Nan Duan[2]

[1]Carnegie Mellon University   [2]Microsoft Research   [3]University of Southern California

{fangzhex, gneubig, ybisk}@cs.cmu.edu

{leiji, nanduan}@microsoft.com

Abstract

Watching instructional videos are often used to learn about procedures. Video captioning is one way of automatically collecting such knowledge. However, it provides only an indirect, overall evaluation of multimodal models with no finer-grained quantitative measure of what they have learned. We propose instead, a benchmark of *structured* procedural knowledge extracted from cooking videos. This work is complementary to existing tasks, but requires models to produce interpretable structured knowledge in the form of verb-argument tuples. Our manually annotated open-vocabulary resource includes 356 instructional cooking videos and 15,523 video clip/sentence-level annotations. Our analysis shows that the proposed task is challenging and standard modeling approaches like unsupervised segmentation, semantic role labeling, and visual action detection perform poorly when forced to predict every action of a procedure in structured form.

1 Introduction

Instructional videos are a convenient way to learn a new skill. Although learning from video seems natural to humans, it requires identifying and understanding procedures and grounding them to the real world. In this paper, we propose a new task and dataset for extracting procedural knowledge into a fine-grained *structured* representation from *multimodal* information contained in a *large-scale* archive of *open-vocabulary* narrative videos with *noisy transcripts*. While there is a significant amount of related work (summarized in §3 & 7), to our knowledge there is no dataset similar in scope, with previous attempts focusing only on a single

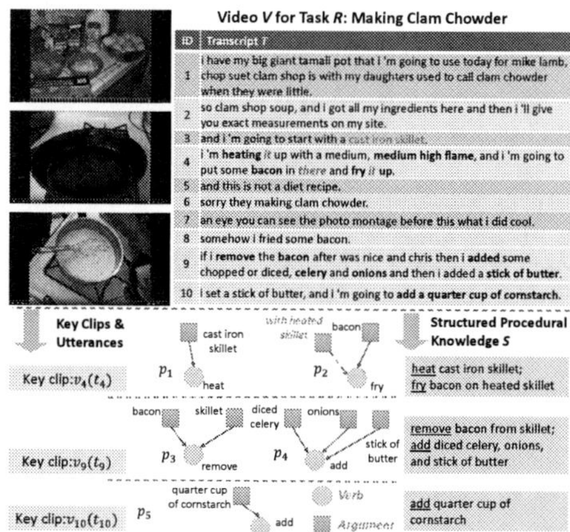

Figure 1: An example of extracting procedures for task *"Making Clam Chowder"*.

modality (e.g., text only (Kiddon et al., 2015) or video only (Zhukov et al., 2019; Alayrac et al., 2016)), using closed-domain taxonomies (Tang et al., 2019), or lacking structure in the procedural representation (Zhou et al., 2018a).

In our task, given a narrative video, say a cooking video on YouTube about *making clam chowder* as shown in Figure 1, our goal is to extract a series of tuples representing the procedure, e.g. (heat, cast iron skillet), (fry, bacon, with heated skillet), etc. We created a manually annotated, large test dataset for evaluation of the task, including over 350 instructional cooking videos along with over 15,000 English sentences in the transcripts spanning over 89 recipe types. This verb-argument structure using arbitrary textual phrases is motivated by open information extraction (Schmitz et al., 2012; Fader et al., 2011), but focuses on procedures rather than entity-entity relations.

This task is challenging with respect to both video and language understanding. For video, it requires understanding of video contents, with a spe-

---

* Work done at Microsoft Research Asia. Data and code: https://github.com/frankxu2004/cooking-procedural-extraction. Full version: https://arxiv.org/abs/2005.00706

Proceedings of the First International Workshop on Natural Language Processing Beyond Text, pages 30–40

Online, November 20, 2020. ©2020 Association for Computational Linguistics

http://www.aclweb.org/anthology/W23-20%2d

cial focus on actions and procedures. For language, it requires understanding of oral narratives, including understanding of predicate-argument structure and coreference. In many cases it is necessary for both modalities to work together, such as when resolving null arguments necessitates the use of objects or actions detected from video contents in addition to transcripts. For example, the cooking video host may say "just a pinch of salt in", while adding some salt into a boiling pot of soup, in which case inferring the action "add" and its argument "pot" requires visual understanding.

Along with the novel task and dataset, we propose several baseline approaches that extract structure in a pipelined fashion. These methods first identify key clips/sentences using video and transcript information with unsupervised and supervised multimodal methods, then extract procedure tuples from the utterances and/or video of these key clips. On the utterances side, we utilize an existing state-of-the-art semantic role labeling model (Shi and Lin, 2019), with the intuition that semantic role labeling captures the verb-argument structures of a sentence, which would be directly related to procedures and actions. On the video side, similarly, we utilize existing state-of-the-art video action/object recognition model trained in kitchen settings to further augment utterance-only extraction results. The results are far from perfect, demonstrating that the proposed task is challenging and that structuring procedures requires more than just state-of-the-art semantic parsing or video action recognition.

2 Problem Definition

We show a concrete example of our procedural knowledge extraction task in Figure 1. Our ultimate goal is to automatically map *unstructured* instructional video (clip and utterances) to *structured* procedures, defining what actions should be performed on which objects, with what arguments and in what order. We define the input to such an extraction system:

- Task R, e.g. "Create Chicken Parmesan" and instructional video V_R describing the procedure to achieve task R, e.g. a video titled "Chicken Parmesan - Let's Cook with ModernMom".[1]
- A sequence of n sentences $T_R = \{t_0, t_1, ..., t_n\}$ representing video V_R's corresponding transcript. According to the time stamps of the

transcript sentences, the video is also segmented into n clips $V_R = \{v_0, v_1, ..., v_n\}$ accordingly to align with the sentences in the transcript T_R.

The output will be:

- A sequence of m procedure tuples $S_R = \{s_0, s_1, ..., s_m\}$ describing the key steps to achieve task R according to instructional video V_R.
- An identified list of *key* video clips and corresponding sentences $V_R' \subseteq V_R$, to which procedures in S_R are grounded.

Each procedural tuple $s_j = (\text{verb}, \text{arg}_1, ..., \text{arg}_k) \in S_R$ consists of a verb phrase and its arguments. Only the "verb" field is required, and thus the tuple size ranges from 1 to $k + 1$. All fields can be either a word or a phrase.

Not every clip/sentence describes procedures, as most videos include an intro, an outro, non-procedural narration, or off-topic chit-chat. Key clips V_R' are clips associated with one or more procedures in P_R, with some clips/sentences associated with multiple procedure tuples. Conversely, each procedure tuple will be associated with only a single clip/sentence.

3 Dataset & Analysis

While others have created related datasets, they fall short on key dimensions which we remedy in our work. Specifically, In Table 1 we compare to AllRecipes (Kiddon et al., 2015) (AR), YouCook2 (Zhou et al., 2018b) (YC2), CrossTask (Zhukov et al., 2019) (CT), COIN (Tang et al., 2019), How2 (Sanabria et al., 2018), HAKE (Li et al., 2019) and TACOS (Regneri et al., 2013). Additional details about datasets are included in the Appendix A.[2] In summary, none have both *structured* and *open* extraction annotations for the procedural knowledge extraction task, since most focus on either video summarization/captioning or action localization/classification.

	Ours	AR	YC2	CT	COIN	How2	HAKE	TACOS
General domain?				✓	✓	✓	✓	
Multimodal input?	✓					✓	✓	✓
Use transcript?	✓					✓		
Use noisy text?	✓					✓		
Open extraction?	✓		✓					
Structured format?	✓	✓		✓			✓	✓

Table 1: Comparison to current datasets.

---

[1] https://www.youtube.com/watch?v=nWGpCmDlNU4

[2] A common dataset we do not include here is HowTo100M (Miech et al., 2019) as it does not contain any annotations.

Figure 2: Annotation interface.

	Verbs	Arguments
Total #	4004	6070
Average # per key clip	1.12	1.70
Average #words	1.07	1.43
% directly from transcript	69.8	75.0
% coreference (pronouns)	N/A	14.4
% ellipsis	30.2	10.6

Table 2: Statistics of annotated verbs and arguments in procedures.

3.1 Dataset Creation

To address the limitations of existing datasets, we created our own evaluation dataset by annotating structured procedure knowledge given the video and transcript. Native English-speakers annotated four videos per recipe type (e.g. clam chowder, pizza margherita, etc.) in the YouCook2 dataset into the structured form presented in §2 (totaling 356 videos). Annotators selected key clips as important steps and extracted corresponding fields to fill in verbs and arguments. Filling in the fields with the original tokens was preferred but not required (e.g., in cases of coreference and ellipsis). The result is a series of video clips labeled with procedural structured knowledge as a sequence of steps s_j and series of short sentences describing the procedure.

Figure 2 shows the user interface of annotation tool. The process is divided into 3 questions per clip: **Q1:** Determine if the video clip is a key step if: (1) the clip or transcript contains at least one action; (2) the action is required for accomplishing the task (i.e. not a self introduction); and (3) for if a clip duplicates a previous key clip, choose the one with clearer visual and textual signals (e.g. without coreference, etc.). **Q2:** For each key video clip, annotate the key procedural tuples. We have

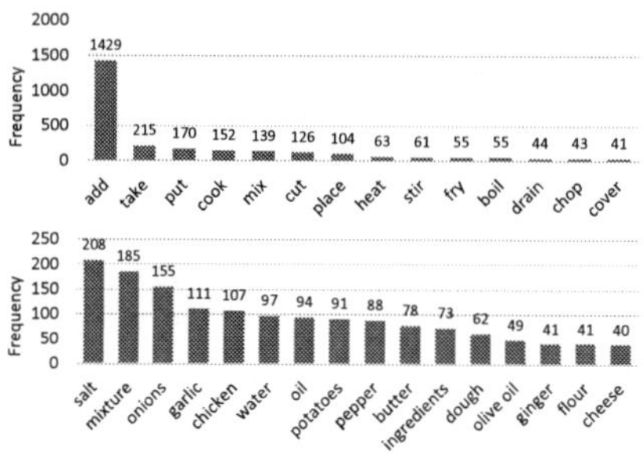

Figure 3: Most frequent verbs (upper) and arguments (lower).

annotators indicate which actions are both seen and mentioned by the instructor in the video. The actions should correspond to a verb and its arguments from the original transcript except in the case of ellipsis or coreference where they have to refer to earlier phrases based on the visual scene. **Q3:** Construct a short fluent sentence from the annotated tuples for the given video clip.

We have two expert annotators and a professional labeling supervisor for quality control and deciding the final annotations. To improve the data quality, the supervisor reviewed all labeling results, and applied several heuristic rules to find anomalous records for further correction. The heuristic is to check the annotated verb/arguments that are not found in corresponding transcript text. Among these anomalies, the supervisor checks the conflicts between the two annotators. 25% of all annotations were modified as a result. On average annotators completed task Q1 at 240 sentences (clips) per hour and task Q2 and Q3 combined at 40 sentences per hour. For Q1, we observe an inter-annotator agreement with Cohen's Kappa of 0.83.[3] Examples are shown in Table 3.

3.2 Dataset Analysis

Overall, the dataset contains 356 videos with 15,523 video clips/sentences, among which 3,569 clips are labeled as key steps. Sentences average 16.3 tokens, and the language style is oral English. For structured procedural annotations, there are 347 unique verbs and 1,237 unique objects in all. Statistics are shown in Table 2. Figure 3 lists the most commonly appearing verbs and entities. The action *add* is most frequently performed, and the entities *salt* and *onions* are the most popular ingredients.

---

[3] We use the Jaccard ratio between the annotated tokens of two annotators for Q2's agreement. Verb annotations have a higher agreement at 0.77 than that of arguments at 0.72.

Transcript sentence	Procedure summary	Verb	Arguments	
so we've **placed the dough directly into the caputo flour** that we import from italy.	place dough in caputo flour	place	dough	caputo flour
we just **give** *(ellipsis)* **a squish with our palm and make** *it* **flat in the center**.	squish dough with palm	squish	dough	with palm
	flatten center of dough	flatten	center of dough	
so will have to **rotate** *it* **every thirty to forty five seconds** ...	rotate pizza every 30-45 seconds	rotate	pizza	every 30-45 seconds

Table 3: Annotations of structured procedures and summaries. *Coreference* and *ellipsis* are marked with *italics* and are resolved into referred phrases also linked back in the annotations. See Appendix (Table 6) for more examples.

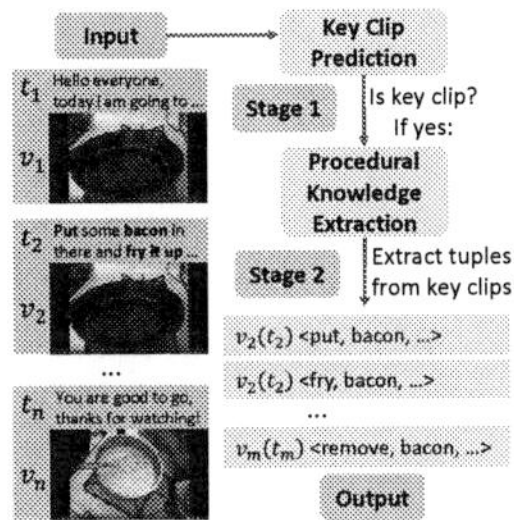

Figure 4: Extraction pipeline.

In nearly 30% of annotations, some verbs and arguments cannot be directly found in the transcript. An example is "(add) some salt into the pot", and we refer to this variety of absence as *ellipsis*. Arguments not mentioned explicitly are mainly due to (1) pronoun references, e.g. "put it (fish) in the pan"; (2) ellipsis, where the arguments are absent from the oral language, e.g. "put the mixture inside" where the argument "oven" is omitted. The details can be found in Table 2. The coreferences and ellipsis phenomena add difficulty to our task, and indicate the utility of using multimodal information from the video signal and contextual procedural knowledge for inference.

4 Extraction Stage 1: Key Clip Selection

In this and the following section, we describe our two-step pipeline for procedural knowledge extraction (also in Figure 4). This section describes the first stage of determining which clips are "key clips" that contribute to the description of the procedure. We describe several key clip selection models, which consume the transcript and/or the video within the clip and decide whether it is a key clip.

4.1 Parsing-Based Heuristic Baselines

Given our unsupervised setting, we first examine two heuristic parsing-based methods that focus on the transcript only, one based on semantic role labeling (SRL) and the other based on an unsupervised segmentation model Kiddon et al. (2015).

Before introducing heuristic baselines, we note that having a lexicon of domain-specific actions will be useful, e.g., for filtering pretrained model outputs, or providing priors to the unsupervised model described later. In our cooking domain, these actions can be expected to consist mostly of verbs related to cooking actions and procedures. Observing recipe datasets such as AllRecipes (Kiddon et al., 2015) or WikiHow (Miech et al., 2019; Zhukov et al., 2019), we find that they usually use imperative and concise sentences for procedures and the first word is usually the action verb like *"add"*, e.g., *add some salt into the pot*. We thus construct a cooking lexicon by aggregating the frequently appearing verbs as the first word from All-Recipes, with frequency over a threshold of 5. We further filter out words that have no verb synsets in WordNet (Miller, 1995). Finally we manually filter out noisy or too general verbs like "go". Note that when applying to other domains, the lexicon can be built following a similar process of first finding a domain-specific corpus with simple and formal instructions, and then obtaining the lexicon by aggregation and filtering.

Semantic role labeling baselines. One intuitive trigger in the transcript for deciding whether the sentence is a key step should be the action words, i.e. the verbs. In order to identify these action words we use semantic role labeling (Gildea and Jurafsky, 2002), which analyzes natural language sentences to extract information about "who did what to whom, when, where and how?" The output is in the form of predicates and their respective arguments that acts as semantic roles, where the verb acts as the root (head) of the parse. We run a strong semantic role labeling model (Shi and Lin, 2019) included in the AllenNLP toolkit (Gardner et al., 2018) on each sentence in the transcript. From the output we get a set of verbs for each of the sentences.[4] Because not all verbs in all sentences represent actual key actions for the procedure, we

---

[4]The SRL model is used in this stage only as a verb identifier, with other output information used in stage 2.

additionally filter the verbs with the heuristically created cooking lexicon above, counting a clip as a key clip only if at least one of the SRL-detected verbs is included in the lexicon.

Unsupervised recipe segmentation baseline (Kiddon et al., 2015). The second baseline is based on the outputs of the unsupervised recipe sentence segmentation model in Kiddon et al. (2015). Briefly speaking, the model is a generative probabilistic model where verbs and arguments, together with their numbers, are modeled as latent variables. It uses a bigram model for string selection. It is trained on the whole transcript corpus of YouCook2 videos iteratively for 15 epochs using a hard EM approach before the performance starts to converge. The count of verbs in the lexicon created in §4.1 is provided as a prior through initialization. We then do inference to parse the transcripts in our dataset using the trained model. Following the same heuristics as the SRL outputs, we treat sentences with non-empty parsed predicates after lexical filtering as key sentences, and those without as negatives.

4.2 Neural Selection Baseline

Next, we implement a supervised neural network model that incorporates visual information, which we have posited before may be useful in the face of incomplete verbal utterances. We extract the features of the sentence and each video frame using pretrained feature extractors respectively. Then we perform attention (Bahdanau et al., 2014) over each frame feature, using the sentence as a query, in order to acquire the representation of the video clip. Finally, we combine the visual and textual features to predict whether the input is a key clip. The model is trained on a *general domain* instructional key clip selection dataset with *no* overlap with ours, and our annotated dataset is used for evaluation *only*. Additional details about the model and training dataset are included in Appendix B.

5 Extraction Stage 2: Structured Knowledge Extraction

With the identified key clips and corresponding transcript sentences, we proceed to the second stage that performs clip/sentence-level procedural knowledge extraction from key clips. In this stage, the extraction is done from clips that are identified at first as "key clips".

5.1 Extraction From Utterances

We first present two baselines to extract structured procedures using transcripts only, similarly to the key-clip identification methods described in §4.1. **Semantic role labeling.** For the first baseline, we use the same pretrained SRL model introduced in §4.1 to conduct inference on the sentences in key clips identified from stage 1. Because they consist of verb-argument structures, the outputs of the SRL model are well aligned with the task of extracting procedural tuples that identify actions and their arguments. However, not all outputs from the SRL model are the structured procedural knowledge we aim to extract. For example, in the sentence *"you 're ready to add a variety of bell peppers"* from the transcript, the outputs from SRL model contains two parses with two predicates, *"are"* and *"add"*, where only the latter is actually part of the procedure. To deal with this issue we first perform filtering similar to that used in stage 1, removing parses with predicates (verbs) outside of the domain-specific action lexicon we created in §4.1. Next, we filter out irrelevant arguments in the parse. For example, the parse from the SRL model for sentence "I add a lot of pepper because I love it." after filtering out irrelevant verb "love" is "[ARG0: I] [V: add] [ARG1: a lot of pepper] [ARGM-CAU: because I love it]", some arguments such as ARG0 and ARGM-CAU are clearly not contributing to the procedure. We provide a complete list of the filtered argument types in Appendix C.

Unsupervised recipe segmentation (Kiddon et al., 2015). The second baseline is to use the same trained segmentation model as in §4.1 to segment selected key transcript sentences into verbs and arguments. We treat segmented predicates in the key sentence as procedural verbs, and segmented predicate arguments plus preposition arguments as procedural arguments.

5.2 Extraction From Video

We also examine a baseline that utilizes two forms of visual information in videos: actions and objects. We predict both verbs and nouns of a given video clip via a state-of-the-art action detection model TSM (Lin et al., 2019),[5] trained on the EpicKitchen (Damen et al., 2018a) dataset.[6] For each video, we extract 5-sec video segments and feed

---

[5] `https://github.com/epic-kitchens/action-models`

[6] `https://epic-kitchens.github.io/2019`

	Acc	P	R	F1
Parsing-based Heuristics				
SRL w/o heur.	25.9	23.4	**97.6**	37.7
SRL w/ heur.	61.2	35.2	81.4	49.1
Kiddon et al. (2015)	67.3	33.5	42.7	37.6
Neural Model				
Visual Only	43.8	27.2	85.9	41.3
Text Only	76.3	49.0	78.1	60.2
V+T (Full Model)	**77.7**	**51.0**	75.3	**60.8**

Table 4: Key clip selection results.

into the action detection model. The outputs of the models are in a *predefined* set of labels of verbs (actions) and nouns (objects).[7] We directly combine the outputs from the model on each video segment, aggregate and temporally align them with key clips/sentences, forming the final output.

5.3 Utterance and Video Fusion

Finally, to take advantage of the fact that utterance and video provide complementary views, we perform multimodal fusion of the results of both of these model varieties. We adopt a simple method of fusion by taking the union of the verbs/actions and arguments/objects respectively from the best performing utterance-only model and the visual detection model.

6 Evaluation

We propose evaluation metrics and provide evaluation results on our annotated dataset for both of the two stages: key clip selection and structured procedural extraction. Detailed reproducibility information about the experiments are in Appendix F. Besides quantitative evaluation and qualitative evaluations, we also analyze the key challenges of this task.

6.1 Extraction Stage 1: Key Clip Selection

In this section, we evaluate results of the key clip selection described in §4. We evaluate using the accuracy, precision, recall and F1 score for the binary classification problem of whether a given clip in the video is a key clip. The results are shown in Table 4. We compare parsing-based heuristic models and supervised neural models, with ablations (model details in Appendix B). From the experimental results in Table 4, we can see that:

1. Unsupervised heuristic methods perform worse than neural models with training data. This is

despite the fact that the dataset used for training neural models has a different data distribution and domain from the test set.

2. Among heuristic methods, pretrained SRL is better than Kiddon et al. (2015) even though the second is trained on transcript text from YouCook2 videos. One possible reason is that the unsupervised segmentation method was specially designed for recipe texts, which are mostly simple, concise and imperative sentences found in recipe books, while the transcript is full of noise and tends to have longer, more complicated, and oral-style English.

3. Post-processing significantly improves the SRL model, showing that filtering unrelated arguments and incorporating the cooking lexicon helps, especially with reducing false positives.

4. Among neural method ablations, the model using only visual features performs worse than that using only text features. The best model for identifying key clips among proposed baselines uses both visual and text information in the neural model.

Besides quantitative evaluation, we analyzed key clip identification results and found a number of observations. First, background introductions, advertisements for the YouTube channel, etc. can be relatively well classified due to major differences both visually and textually from procedural clips. Second, alignment and grounding between the visual and textual domains is crucial for key clip prediction, yet challenging. For example, the clip with the transcript sentence "add more pepper according to your liking" is identified as a key clip. However, it is in fact merely a suggestion made by the speaker about an imaginary scenario, rather than a real action performed and thus should not be regarded as a key procedure.

6.2 Extraction Stage 2: Structured Procedure Extraction

In this stage, we perform key clip-level evaluation for structured procedural knowledge extraction by matching the ground truth and predicted structures with both exact match and two fuzzy scoring strategies. To better show how stage 1 performance affects the whole pipeline, we evaluate on both ground truth (oracle) and predicted key clips. Similarly to the evaluation of key clip selection, we compare the parsing-based methods (§5.1), as well as purposing the action detection results from

---

[7]Notably, this contrasts to our setting of attempting to recognize into an open label set, which upper-bounds the accuracy of any model with a limited label set.

| Model | Verbs | | | | | | | | | Arguments | | | | | | | | |
| | Exact Match | | | Fuzzy | | | Partial Fuzzy | | | Exact Match | | | Fuzzy | | | Partial Fuzzy | | |
	P	R	F1	P	R	F1	P	R	F1	P	R	F1	P	R	F1	P	R	F1
Using oracle key clips																		
Kiddon et al. (2015)	12.0	10.9	11.4	18.8	17.2	18.0	20.2	18.4	19.3	0.4	0.9	0.5	10.4	19.3	13.5	16.4	30.2	21.3
SRL w/o heur.	19.4	54.7	28.6	25.3	70.1	37.2	26.6	73.8	39.1	1.3	**5.4**	2.0	14.1	**53.6**	22.3	22.0	**81.8**	34.6
SRL w/ heur.	**38.7**	51.6	**44.3**	**45.2**	60.3	**51.7**	**46.9**	62.6	**53.6**	**1.6**	3.3	**2.2**	**21.2**	39.8	**27.7**	**32.3**	59.5	**41.9**
Visual	4.1	6.7	5.1	17.9	27.8	21.7	19.3	30.1	23.5	0.9	1.1	1.0	17.8	25.8	21.1	24.2	36.2	29.0
Fusion	19.9	**55.2**	29.3	28.6	**73.3**	41.2	31.2	**78.6**	44.7	1.1	3.8	1.6	16.9	50.0	25.2	24.4	72.5	36.5
Using predicted key clips																		
Kiddon et al. (2015)	7.0	6.3	6.6	10.9	10.0	10.4	11.7	10.7	11.2	0.2	0.5	0.3	6.1	11.2	7.9	9.5	17.5	12.3
SRL w/o heur.	11.2	31.7	16.6	14.7	40.7	21.6	15.4	42.8	22.6	0.7	**3.1**	1.2	8.2	**31.1**	13.0	12.7	**47.4**	20.1
SRL w/ heur.	**22.5**	29.9	**25.7**	**26.2**	35.0	**30.0**	**27.2**	36.3	**31.1**	**0.9**	1.9	**1.3**	**12.3**	23.1	**16.1**	**18.8**	34.5	**24.3**
Visual	2.4	3.9	3.0	10.4	16.1	12.6	11.2	17.5	13.7	0.5	0.6	0.6	10.3	15.0	12.2	14.1	21.0	16.8
Fusion	11.5	**32.0**	17.0	16.6	**42.5**	23.9	18.1	**45.6**	25.9	0.6	2.2	1.0	9.8	29.0	14.6	14.1	42.1	21.2

Table 5: Clip/sentence-level structured procedure extraction results for verbs and arguments.

video signals for our task. Besides, we compare utterance-only and video-only baselines with our naive multi-modal fusion method.

We evaluate with respect to precision, recall and the F1 measure. Similarly to the evaluation method used for SRL (Carreras and Màrquez, 2004), precision (P) is the proportion of verbs or arguments predicted by a model which are correct, i.e. $TP/\#$predicted where TP is the number of true positives. Recall (R) is the proportion of correct verbs or arguments which are predicted by a model, i.e. $TP/\#$gold. The key here is how to calculate TP and we propose 3 methods: exact match, fuzzy matching, and partial fuzzy matching. The first is straight forward, we count true positives if and only if the predicted phrase is an exact string match in the gold phrases. However, because our task lies in the realm of open phrase extraction without predefined labels, it is unfairly strict to count only the exact string matches as TP. Also by design, the gold extraction results cannot always be found in the original transcript sentence (refer to §3.2), so we are also unable to use token-based metrics as in sequence tagging (Sang and De Meulder, 2003), or span-based metrics as in some question answering tasks (Rajpurkar et al., 2016). Thus for the second metric we call *"fuzzy"*, we leverage edit distance to enable fuzzy matching and assign a "soft" score for TP. In some cases, the two strings of quite different lengths will hurt the *fuzzy* score due to the nature of edit distance, even though one string is a substring of another. To get around this, we propose a third metric, *"partial fuzzy"* to get the score of the best matching substring with the length of the shorter string in comparison. Note that this third metric will bias towards shorter, correct phrases and thus we should have a holistic view of all 3 metrics during the evaluation. Details of two fuzzy metrics are described in Appendix D.

Table 5 illustrates evaluation results:

1. Argument extraction is much more challenging compared to verb extraction, according the results: arguments contain more complex types of phrases (e.g. objects, location, time, etc.) and are longer in length. It is hard to identify complex arguments with our current heuristic or unsupervised baselines and thus the need for better supervised or semi-supervised models.

2. Heuristic SRL methods perform better than the unsupervised segmentation model even though the second is trained on our corpus. This demonstrates the generality of SRL models, but the heuristics applied at the output of SRL models still improve the performance by reducing false positives.

3. The visual-only method performs the worst, mainly because of the domain gap between visual detection model outputs and our annotated verbs and arguments. Other reasons include: the closed label set predefined in EpicKitchen; challenges in domain transferring from closed to open extraction; different video data distribution between EpicKitchen (for training) and our dataset (YouCook2, for testing); limited performance of video detection model itself.

4. Naive multimodal fusion leads to an overall performance drop to below the utterance-only model, partly due to the differences in video data distribution and domain, as well as the limitation of the predefined set of verbs and nouns in the EpicKitchen dataset, implying the need for better multimodal fusion method. Unsurprisingly, the recall for verb extraction raises after the fusion, suggesting that action detection in videos helps with the coverage. The drop in argument extraction suggests the complexity of arguments in our open extraction setting: it

should be more than mere object detection.

Besides quantitative results, we also showcase qualitative analysis of example extraction outputs in Appendix E. From both, we suggest that there are two key challenges moving forward:

Verb extraction: We find that verb ellipsis is common in transcripts. The transcript text contains sentences where key action "verbs" do not have verb part-of-speech in the sentence. For example, in the sentence "give it a flip ..." with the annotation ("flip", "pancake"), the model detects "give" as the verb rather than "flip". Currently all our baselines are highly reliant on a curated lexicon for verb selection and thus such cases will get filtered out. How to deal with such cases with general verbs like *make*, *give*, *do* remains challenging and requires extracting from the contexts.

Argument extraction: Speech-to-text errors are intrinsic in automatically acquired transcripts and cause problems during parsing that cascade. Examples are that "add flour" being recognized as "add flower" and "sriracha sauce" being recognized as "sarrah cha sauce" causing wrong extraction outputs. Coreference and ellipsis are also challenging and hurting current benchmark performance, as our baselines do not tackle any of these explicitly. Visual co-reference and language grounding (Huang et al., 2018, 2017) provides a feasible method for us to tackle these cases in the future.

7 Related Work

Text-based procedural knowledge extraction. Procedural text understanding and knowledge extraction (Chu et al., 2017; Park and Motahari Nezhad, 2018; Kiddon et al., 2015; Jermsurawong and Habash, 2015; Liu et al., 2016; Long et al., 2016; Maeta et al., 2015; Malmaud et al., 2014; Artzi and Zettlemoyer, 2013; Kuehne et al., 2017) has been studied for years on step-wise textual data such as WikiHow. Chu et al. (2017) extracted open-domain knowledge from how-to communities. Recently Zhukov et al. (2019) also studied to adopt the well-written how-to data as weak supervision for instructional video understanding. Unlike existing work on action graph/dependency extraction (Kiddon et al., 2015; Jermsurawong and Habash, 2015), our approach differs as we extract knowledge from the visual signals and transcripts directly, not from imperative recipe texts.

Instructional video understanding. Beyond image semantics (Yatskar et al., 2016), unlike existing tasks for learning from instructional video (Zhou et al., 2018c; Tang et al., 2019; Alayrac et al., 2016; Song et al., 2015; Sener et al., 2015; Huang et al., 2016; Sun et al., 2019b,a; Plummer et al., 2017; Palaskar et al., 2019), combining video & text information in procedures (Yagcioglu et al., 2018; Fried et al., 2020), visual-linguistic reference resolution (Huang et al., 2018, 2017), visual planning (Chang et al., 2019), joint learning of object and actions (Zhukov et al., 2019; Richard et al., 2018; Gao et al., 2017; Damen et al., 2018b), pretraining joint embedding of high level sentence with video clips (Sun et al., 2019b; Miech et al., 2019), our task proposal requires explicit structured knowledge tuple extraction.

In addition to closely related work (§3) there is a wide literature (Malmaud et al., 2015; Zhou et al., 2018b; Ushiku et al., 2017; Nishimura et al., 2019; Tang et al., 2019; Huang et al., 2016; Shi et al., 2019; Ushiku et al., 2017) that aims to predict/align dense procedural captions given the video, which are the most similar works to ours. Zhou et al. (2018c) extracted temporal procedures and then generated captioning for each procedure. Sanabria et al. (2018) proposes a multimodal abstractive summarization for how-to videos with either human labeled or speech-to-text transcript. Alayrac et al. (2016) also introduces an unsupervised step learning method from instructional videos. Inspired by cross-task sharing (Zhukov et al., 2019), which is a weakly supervised method to learn shared actions between tasks, fine grained action and entity are important for sharing similar knowledge between various tasks. We focus on *structured* knowledge of fine-grained actions and entities.Visual-linguistic coreference resolution (Huang et al., 2018, 2017) is among one of the open challenges for our proposed task.

8 Conclusions & Open Challenges

We propose a multimodal open procedural knowledge extraction task, present a new evaluation dataset, produce benchmarks with various methods, and analyze the difficulties in the task. Meanwhile we investigate the limit of existing methods and many open challenges for procedural knowledge acquisition, including: to better deal with cases of coreference and ellipsis in visual-grounded languages; exploit cross-modalities of information with more robust, semi/un-supervised models; potential improvement from structured knowledge in downstream tasks (e.g., video captioning).

References

Jean-Baptiste Alayrac, Piotr Bojanowski, Nishant Agrawal, Josef Sivic, Ivan Laptev, and Simon Lacoste-Julien. 2016. Unsupervised learning from narrated instruction videos. In *Proceedings of the IEEE Conference on Computer Vision and Pattern Recognition*, pages 4575–4583.

Yoav Artzi and Luke Zettlemoyer. 2013. Weakly supervised learning of semantic parsers for mapping instructions to actions. *Transactions of the Association for Computational Linguistics*, 1:49–62.

Dzmitry Bahdanau, Kyunghyun Cho, and Yoshua Bengio. 2014. Neural machine translation by jointly learning to align and translate. *arXiv preprint arXiv:1409.0473*.

Xavier Carreras and Lluís Màrquez. 2004. Introduction to the conll-2004 shared task: Semantic role labeling. In *Proceedings of the Eighth Conference on Computational Natural Language Learning (CoNLL-2004) at HLT-NAACL 2004*, pages 89–97.

Chien-Yi Chang, De-An Huang, Danfei Xu, Ehsan Adeli, Li Fei-Fei, and Juan Carlos Niebles. 2019. Procedure planning in instructional videos. *ArXiv*, abs/1907.01172.

Cuong Xuan Chu, Niket Tandon, and Gerhard Weikum. 2017. Distilling task knowledge from how-to communities. In *Proceedings of the 26th International Conference on World Wide Web*, pages 805–814. International World Wide Web Conferences Steering Committee.

Dima Damen, Hazel Doughty, Giovanni Maria Farinella, Sanja Fidler, Antonino Furnari, Evangelos Kazakos, Davide Moltisanti, Jonathan Munro, Toby Perrett, Will Price, and Michael Wray. 2018a. Scaling egocentric vision: The epic-kitchens dataset. In *European Conference on Computer Vision (ECCV)*.

Dima Damen, Hazel Doughty, Giovanni Maria Farinella, Sanja Fidler, Antonino Furnari, Evangelos Kazakos, Davide Moltisanti, Jonathan Munro, Toby Perrett, Will Price, et al. 2018b. Scaling egocentric vision: The epic-kitchens dataset. In *Proceedings of the European Conference on Computer Vision (ECCV)*, pages 720–736.

Jia Deng, Wei Dong, Richard Socher, Li-Jia Li, Kai Li, and Li Fei-Fei. 2009. Imagenet: A large-scale hierarchical image database. In *2009 IEEE conference on computer vision and pattern recognition*, pages 248–255. Ieee.

Jacob Devlin, Ming-Wei Chang, Kenton Lee, and Kristina Toutanova. 2018. Bert: Pre-training of deep bidirectional transformers for language understanding. *arXiv preprint arXiv:1810.04805*.

Anthony Fader, Stephen Soderland, and Oren Etzioni. 2011. Identifying relations for open information extraction. In *Proceedings of the conference on empirical methods in natural language processing*, pages 1535–1545. Association for Computational Linguistics.

Daniel Fried, Jean-Baptiste Alayrac, Phil Blunsom, Chris Dyer, Stephen Clark, and Aida Nematzadeh. 2020. Learning to segment actions from observation and narration.

Jiyang Gao, Chen Sun, Zhenheng Yang, and Ram Nevatia. 2017. Tall: Temporal activity localization via language query. In *Proceedings of the IEEE International Conference on Computer Vision*, pages 5267–5275.

Matt Gardner, Joel Grus, Mark Neumann, Oyvind Tafjord, Pradeep Dasigi, Nelson Liu, Matthew Peters, Michael Schmitz, and Luke Zettlemoyer. 2018. Allennlp: A deep semantic natural language processing platform. *arXiv preprint arXiv:1803.07640*.

Daniel Gildea and Daniel Jurafsky. 2002. Automatic labeling of semantic roles. *Computational linguistics*, 28(3):245–288.

Kaiming He, Xiangyu Zhang, Shaoqing Ren, and Jian Sun. 2016. Deep residual learning for image recognition. In *Proceedings of the IEEE conference on computer vision and pattern recognition*, pages 770–778.

De-An Huang, Shyamal Buch, Lucio Dery, Animesh Garg, Li Fei-Fei, and Juan Carlos Niebles. 2018. Finding "it": Weakly-supervised, reference-aware visual grounding in instructional videos. In *IEEE Conference on Computer Vision and Pattern Recognition (CVPR)*.

De-An Huang, Li Fei-Fei, and Juan Carlos Niebles. 2016. Connectionist temporal modeling for weakly supervised action labeling. In *European Conference on Computer Vision*, pages 137–153. Springer.

De-An Huang, Joseph J Lim, Li Fei-Fei, and Juan Carlos Niebles. 2017. Unsupervised visual-linguistic reference resolution in instructional videos. In *Proceedings of the IEEE Conference on Computer Vision and Pattern Recognition*, pages 2183–2192.

Jermsak Jermsurawong and Nizar Habash. 2015. Predicting the structure of cooking recipes. In *Proceedings of the 2015 Conference on Empirical Methods in Natural Language Processing*, pages 781–786.

Chloé Kiddon, Ganesa Thandavam Ponnuraj, Luke S. Zettlemoyer, and Yejin Choi. 2015. Mise en place: Unsupervised interpretation of instructional recipes. In *EMNLP*.

Diederik P Kingma and Jimmy Ba. 2014. Adam: A method for stochastic optimization. *arXiv preprint arXiv:1412.6980*.

Hilde Kuehne, Alexander Richard, and Juergen Gall. 2017. Weakly supervised learning of actions from transcripts. *Computer Vision and Image Understanding*, 163:78–89.

Yong-Lu Li, Liang Xu, Xijie Huang, Xinpeng Liu, Ze Ma, Mingyang Chen, Shiyi Wang, Hao-Shu Fang, and Cewu Lu. 2019. Hake: Human activity knowledge engine. *arXiv preprint arXiv:1904.06539*.

Ji Lin, Chuang Gan, and Song Han. 2019. Tsm: Temporal shift module for efficient video understanding. In *Proceedings of the IEEE International Conference on Computer Vision*.

Changsong Liu, Shaohua Yang, Sari Saba-Sadiya, Nishant Shukla, Yunzhong He, Song-Chun Zhu, and Joyce Chai. 2016. Jointly learning grounded task structures from language instruction and visual demonstration. In *Proceedings of the 2016 Conference on Empirical Methods in Natural Language Processing*, pages 1482–1492.

Reginald Long, Panupong Pasupat, and Percy Liang. 2016. Simpler context-dependent logical forms via model projections. *arXiv preprint arXiv:1606.05378*.

Hirokuni Maeta, Tetsuro Sasada, and Shinsuke Mori. 2015. A framework for procedural text understanding. In *Proceedings of the 14th International Conference on Parsing Technologies*, pages 50–60.

Jonathan Malmaud, Jonathan Huang, Vivek Rathod, Nicholas Johnston, Andrew Rabinovich, and Kevin Murphy. 2015. What's cookin'? interpreting cooking videos using text, speech and vision. In *Proceedings of the 2015 Conference of the North American Chapter of the Association for Computational Linguistics: Human Language Technologies*, pages 143–152, Denver, Colorado. Association for Computational Linguistics.

Jonathan Malmaud, Earl Wagner, Nancy Chang, and Kevin Murphy. 2014. Cooking with semantics. In *Proceedings of the ACL 2014 Workshop on Semantic Parsing*, pages 33–38.

Antoine Miech, Dimitri Zhukov, Jean-Baptiste Alayrac, Makarand Tapaswi, Ivan Laptev, and Josef Sivic. 2019. HowTo100M: Learning a Text-Video Embedding by Watching Hundred Million Narrated Video Clips. *arXiv:1906.03327*.

George A Miller. 1995. Wordnet: a lexical database for english. *Communications of the ACM*, 38(11):39–41.

James Munkres. 1957. Algorithms for the assignment and transportation problems. *Journal of the society for industrial and applied mathematics*, 5(1):32–38.

Taichi Nishimura, Atsushi Hashimoto, Yoko Yamakata, and Shinsuke Mori. 2019. Frame selection for producing recipe with pictures from an execution video of a recipe. In *Proceedings of the 11th Workshop on Multimedia for Cooking and Eating Activities*, pages 9–16. ACM.

Shruti Palaskar, Jindrich Libovický, Spandana Gella, and Florian Metze. 2019. Multimodal abstractive summarization for how2 videos. *arXiv preprint arXiv:1906.07901*.

Hogun Park and Hamid Reza Motahari Nezhad. 2018. Learning procedures from text: Codifying how-to procedures in deep neural networks. In *Companion Proceedings of the The Web Conference 2018*, pages 351–358. International World Wide Web Conferences Steering Committee.

Bryan A Plummer, Matthew Brown, and Svetlana Lazebnik. 2017. Enhancing video summarization via vision-language embedding. In *Proceedings of the IEEE Conference on Computer Vision and Pattern Recognition*, pages 5781–5789.

Pranav Rajpurkar, Jian Zhang, Konstantin Lopyrev, and Percy Liang. 2016. Squad: 100,000+ questions for machine comprehension of text. *arXiv preprint arXiv:1606.05250*.

Michaela Regneri, Marcus Rohrbach, Dominikus Wetzel, Stefan Thater, Bernt Schiele, and Manfred Pinkal. 2013. Grounding action descriptions in videos. *Transactions of the Association for Computational Linguistics*, 1:25–36.

Alexander Richard, Hilde Kuehne, and Juergen Gall. 2018. Action sets: Weakly supervised action segmentation without ordering constraints. In *Proceedings of the IEEE Conference on Computer Vision and Pattern Recognition*, pages 5987–5996.

Ramon Sanabria, Ozan Caglayan, Shruti Palaskar, Desmond Elliott, Loïc Barrault, Lucia Specia, and Florian Metze. 2018. How2: a large-scale dataset for multimodal language understanding. *arXiv preprint arXiv:1811.00347*.

Erik F Sang and Fien De Meulder. 2003. Introduction to the conll-2003 shared task: Language-independent named entity recognition. *arXiv preprint cs/0306050*.

Michael Schmitz, Robert Bart, Stephen Soderland, Oren Etzioni, et al. 2012. Open language learning for information extraction. In *Proceedings of the 2012 Joint Conference on Empirical Methods in Natural Language Processing and Computational Natural Language Learning*, pages 523–534. Association for Computational Linguistics.

Ozan Sener, Amir R Zamir, Silvio Savarese, and Ashutosh Saxena. 2015. Unsupervised semantic parsing of video collections. In *Proceedings of the IEEE International Conference on Computer Vision*, pages 4480–4488.

Botian Shi, Lei Ji, Yaobo Liang, Nan Duan, Peng Chen, Zhendong Niu, and Ming Zhou. 2019. Dense procedure captioning in narrated instructional videos. In *Proceedings of the 57th Conference of the Association for Computational Linguistics*, pages 6382–6391.

Peng Shi and Jimmy Lin. 2019. Simple bert models for relation extraction and semantic role labeling. *arXiv preprint arXiv:1904.05255*.

Yale Song, Jordi Vallmitjana, Amanda Stent, and Alejandro Jaimes. 2015. Tvsum: Summarizing web videos using titles. In *Proceedings of the IEEE conference on computer vision and pattern recognition*, pages 5179–5187.

Chen Sun, Fabien Baradel, Kevin Murphy, and Cordelia Schmid. 2019a. Learning video representations using contrastive bidirectional transformer.

Chen Sun, Austin Myers, Carl Vondrick, Kevin Murphy, and Cordelia Schmid. 2019b. Videobert: A joint model for video and language representation learning. *arXiv preprint arXiv:1904.01766*.

Yansong Tang, Dajun Ding, Yongming Rao, Yu Zheng, Danyang Zhang, Lili Zhao, Jiwen Lu, and Jie Zhou. 2019. Coin: A large-scale dataset for comprehensive instructional video analysis. In *Proceedings of the IEEE Conference on Computer Vision and Pattern Recognition*, pages 1207–1216.

Atsushi Ushiku, Hayato Hashimoto, Atsushi Hashimoto, and Shinsuke Mori. 2017. Procedural text generation from an execution video. In *Proceedings of the Eighth International Joint Conference on Natural Language Processing (Volume 1: Long Papers)*, pages 326–335, Taipei, Taiwan. Asian Federation of Natural Language Processing.

Semih Yagcioglu, Aykut Erdem, Erkut Erdem, and Nazli Ikizler-Cinbis. 2018. RecipeQA: A challenge dataset for multimodal comprehension of cooking recipes. In *Proceedings of the 2018 Conference on Empirical Methods in Natural Language Processing*, pages 1358–1368, Brussels, Belgium. Association for Computational Linguistics.

Mark Yatskar, Luke Zettlemoyer, and Ali Farhadi. 2016. Situation recognition: Visual semantic role labeling for image understanding. In *Conference on Computer Vision and Pattern Recognition*.

Luowei Zhou, Nathan Louis, and Jason J Corso. 2018a. Weakly-supervised video object grounding from text by loss weighting and object interaction. *arXiv preprint arXiv:1805.02834*.

Luowei Zhou, Chenliang Xu, and Jason J Corso. 2018b. Towards automatic learning of procedures from web instructional videos. In *Thirty-Second AAAI Conference on Artificial Intelligence*.

Luowei Zhou, Yingbo Zhou, Jason J Corso, Richard Socher, and Caiming Xiong. 2018c. End-to-end dense video captioning with masked transformer. In *Proceedings of the IEEE Conference on Computer Vision and Pattern Recognition*, pages 8739–8748.

Dimitri Zhukov, Jean-Baptiste Alayrac, Ramazan Gokberk Cinbis, David Fouhey, Ivan Laptev, and Josef Sivic. 2019. Cross-task weakly supervised learning from instructional videos. In *Computer Vision and Pattern Recognition (CVPR)*.

IESTAC: English-Italian Parallel Corpus for End-to-End Speech-to-Text Machine Translation

Giuseppe Della Corte and **Sara Stymne**
Department of Linguistics and Philology
Uppsala University
giuseppe.dellacorte.1888@student.uu.se
sara.stymne@lingfil.uu.se

Abstract

We discuss a set of methods for the creation of IESTAC: a English-Italian speech and text parallel corpus designed for the training of end-to-end speech-to-text machine translation models and publicly released as part of this work. We first mapped English LibriVox audiobooks and their corresponding English Gutenberg Project e-books to Italian e-books with a set of three complementary methods. Then we aligned the English and the Italian texts using both traditional Gale-Church based alignment methods and a recently proposed tool to perform bilingual sentences alignment computing the cosine similarity of multilingual sentence embeddings. Finally, we forced the alignment between the English audiobooks and the English side of our textual parallel corpus with a text-to-speech and dynamic time warping based forced alignment tool. For each step, we provide the reader with a critical discussion based on detailed evaluation and comparison of the results of the different methods.

1 Introduction

Traditionally, most research on machine translation has been concerned with text-to-text systems. However, there is an increasing interest in speech translation. Speech translation usually refers to the task of translating source language audio signals into a text spoken in a target language. Traditionally, it has been tackled by cascaded ST (speech translation) models that concatenates three technologies: ASR (automatic speech recognition), MT (machine translation), and TTS (text-to-speech). Latency and error propagation are two intrinsic drawbacks of cascaded ST models (Ruiz et al., 2017).

End-to-end speech-to-text machine translation, usually also referred to as direct speech translation, avoid error propagation and reduce latency by directly translating source language audio signals into target language texts. A variety of end-to-end machine and deep learning architectures (Bérard et al., 2016; Weiss et al., 2017; Bérard et al., 2018; Anastasopoulos and Chiang, 2018; Di Gangi et al., 2019b) have been proposed to infer patterns from a first sequence (source language audio utterances) and a second sequence (target language textual translations). Training these models require a large amount of source language audio utterances paired up with their textual translations. Furthermore, since pre-training the encoder on ASR seems to improve the quality of the ST results (Bérard et al., 2018; Di Gangi et al., 2019b), the training data should preferably also include source language audio utterances paired up with their transcriptions.

We discuss the creation of IESTAC (Italian-English Speech and Text Audiobooks Corpus), designed for training English-to-Italian speech-to-text machine translation models. It is publicly available[1] and composed of around 130 hours of English speech aligned with its transcription and Italian textual translation at a sentence level. For a more detailed description of the corpus, see also Della Corte (2020). Our objective is to provide the readers with a methodological contribution for the creation of corpora designed for end-to-end speech-to-text machine translation training. We describe a pipeline to semi-automatically collect audio-textual data from the web and automatically align them. Alignment is performed as a two step process. We first perform bilingual sentences alignment between the English text and its Italian textual translation. Then we force the alignment between the English audio and the English text already aligned with its Italian textual translation. For each step we discuss different possible tools, and evaluate the results, allowing us to give recommendations for tools to use for creating new corpora for other languages.

---

[1]https://github.com/
Giuseppe-Della-Corte/IESTAC

41

Proceedings of the First International Workshop on Natural Language Processing Beyond Text, pages 41–50
Online, November 20, 2020. ©2020 Association for Computational Linguistics
http://www.aclweb.org/anthology/W23-20%2d

2 Related Work

There have been some previous work on creating resources for end-to-end speech-to-text machine translation (Kocabiyikoglu et al., 2018; Di Gangi et al., 2019a; Iranzo-Sánchez et al., 2020; Wang et al., 2020a,b). There are also other related efforts, including computational language documentation for low-resource languages (Godard et al., 2018), multilingual speech corpora creation (Black, 2019), and multi-modal corpora creation (Sanabria et al., 2018). Godard et al. (2018) created a speech-to-text corpus of 5 thousands triplets of Mboshi speech, Mboshi transcription, and French textual translations. Speech elicitation from text was done manually by three qualified speakers. Black (2019) created a large corpus of aligned text, speech, and pronounciation for 700 languages, with texts from the bible. The average duration for each language is 2 hours. Sanabria et al. (2018) created a multi-modal corpus by aligning at a word-level 2000 hours of English instructional YouTube videos with their subtitles. Portuguese textual translations were added by paying bilingual English-Portuguese speakers. Augmented LibriSpeech (Kocabiyikoglu et al., 2018) seem to be the first corpus designed for training end-to-end English-to-French speech-to-text machine translation systems. It was created by collecting public domain audiobooks and e-books from the web and automatically align them. A similar approach was used by Beilharz et al. (2020) to create LibriVoxDeEn, a corpus for German-to-English speech translation. Most recent works have been focused on multilingual corpora creation for speech-to-text machine translation: MuST-C (Di Gangi et al., 2019a), Europarl-ST, CoVoST (Wang et al., 2020a) and CoVoST2 (Wang et al., 2020b)

2.1 Augmented LibriSpeech

LibriSpeech (Panayotov et al., 2015) is a corpus for English ASR, created by aligning English audiobooks from the LibriVox project (Kearns, 2014) with their source English e-books from the Gutenberg Project (Stroube, 2003). It was designed to prioritize speaker variety: it contains only a few audio segments per chapter, and a few chapters per book. Augmented LibriSpeech (Kocabiyikoglu et al., 2018) is an augmentation of LibriSpeech with French textual translations. Kocabiyikoglu et al. (2018) used part of the LibriSpeech metadata (around 1500 English e-book titles) to retrieve their corresponding French e-book titles by querying Dbpedia (Auer et al., 2007). They then compared the retrieved French e-book titles against a web index containing public domain French e-books. The collected English and French e-books were aligned with hunalign (Varga et al., 2007), resulting in a textual parallel corpus. Finally, the English side of the parallel corpus was aligned with the LibriSpeech English audio recordings with Gentle[2].

2.2 MuST-C

Data were collected from the English TED website[3]. Di Gangi et al. (2019a) selected those talks that include both a transcription and a textual translation in German, Spanish, French, Italian, Dutch, Portuguese, Romanian or Russian. MuST-C is split in different data-sets for each language direction. Each data-set contains at least 395 hours of English audio utterances aligned with their transcription and their textual translations. Di Gangi et al. (2019a) used the Gargantua sentence alignment tool (Braune and Fraser, 2010) to perform bilingual sentence alignment between transcripts and textual translations. Then, they forced the alignment between the English audio and the English side of the textual parallel corpora with Gentle.

2.3 Europarl-ST

Europarl-ST (Iranzo-Sánchez et al., 2020) is a multilingual corpus for speech-to-text machine translation in 30 language pairs directions from 6 European languages. Data were collected from the LinkedEP database (Van Aggelen et al., 2017), retrieving the European Parliament debates hold between 2008 and 2012 with their transcriptions, time-spans, and translations. The main focus of Iranzo-Sánchez et al. (2020) was to filter out inaccurate labeled EP speeches. To do so, they performed speaker diarization (SD) for each speech and then forced the speech-to-text alignment at a intra-word sentence granularity. Then, they used the character error rate metrics (CER) to further filter out inaccurate transcribed speeches.

2.4 CoVoST and CoVoST2

Facebook AI[4] recently released CoVoST(Wang et al., 2020a) and CoVoST2 (Wang et al., 2020b). Each CoVoST corpus is an augmentation of CoVo

---

[2]https://github.com/lowerquality/gentle
[3]https://www.ted.com/
[4]https://ai.facebook.com/

(Ardila et al., 2020), a multilingual speech recognition corpus. CoVo already provides pairs of aligned audio and transcription. Wang et al. (2020a) selected 11 languages from Common Voice. Then, they paid professional translators to translate 11 Common Voice data-sets (one for each selected language) into English. In order to ensure the quality of the translations, Wang et al. (2020a) applied different sanity checks to find weak translations and send them back to the professional translators. Interestingly, one of those sanity checks was to compute similarity scores between the sentence embeddings of the source language texts and their translations. By using the same approach, Wang et al. (2020b) released CoVoST2, an extension of CoVoST. It covers training data for end-to-end speech-to-text machine translation for 21 languages to English and for English to 15 languages.

2.5 Corpora and licences

The MuST-C corpus licence (Creative Commons Attribution-NonCommercial-NoDerivs 4.0) does not permit commercial use and prevent derivative works. The Europarl-ST corpus licence (Attribution-NonCommercial 4.0 International license) permits derivative works but it does not allow commercial use. In contrast, the CoVoST corpora have been released under the CC0 licence, while Augmented LibriSpeech has been released under the CC BY 4.0 licence. Both the CC0 and the CC BY 4.0 licences allow commercial use and permit derivative works.

3 Corpus Creation

Due to the fact that we are interested in releasing a freely available corpus with a permissive licence, we mainly follow the approach proposed by Kocabiyikoglu et al. (2018):

- Text collection: collect English audiobooks, English e-books, and their corresponding Italian e-books
- Bilingual sentence alignment: automatically create a parallel corpus aligned at a sentence level from the English and the Italian e-books
- Forced alignment: force the alignment between the English audio segments and the English side of the parallel corpus

4 Text Collection

Our first challenge was to identify freely available Italian e-books corresponding to available English e-books. As a starting point, we used part of the LibriSpeech metadata, more specifically the list of the Gutenberg Project English e-books titles. Sometimes it might happen that a single book was published several times with different titles. Therefore, we pre-processed the English titles list using regular expressions to increase the number of possible titles. We manually found patterns that indicate the presence of alternative titles, subtitles, or publication specific information. These patterns were used to augment the possible titles. For instance, many Gutenberg Project English e-book titles contained two or more possible titles separated by the sub-string , or, (e.g. "Tom Swift and His Sky Racer, or, the Quickest Flight on Record"). At the end of the pre-processing step, the list of English titles was augmented with the inclusion of "Tom Swift and His Sky Racer" and "The Quickest Flight on Record" as two individual list elements.

4.1 Methods

We experimented with three methods for the e-book title translations retrieval task: querying WikiData (Vrandečić and Krötzsch, 2014), querying the Wiki-Media endpoint, automatic machine translation with Google Translate WikiData is a knowledge base containing entities (or objects). Each entity is identified by language labels and alternative labels. Each entity belongs to one or more classes and has a set of properties. As a first method, we wrote a SPARQL query search to retrieve all Wiki-Data objects belonging to the class "literary work" and with an English label, an Italian label, plus, if available, the list of alternative Italian and English labels. English and Italian labels and alternative labels correspond to English and Italian book titles. We then compared the results returned by our SPARQL queries against the LibriSpeech English titles list (see Section 4), returning only those WikiData results which English label (or one of the alternative labels) matched one of the items in LibriSpeech English titles list. Our second method was to identify possible Italian e-books titles by querying each element of the LibriSpeech English e-books titles through the WikiMedia endpoint, returning the Italian web page title corresponding to the English e-book title queried and successfully found to match an English web page from one of the WikiMedia Foundation[5] websites. Our third and final method was to use Google Translate for

---

[5] https://wikimediafoundation.org/

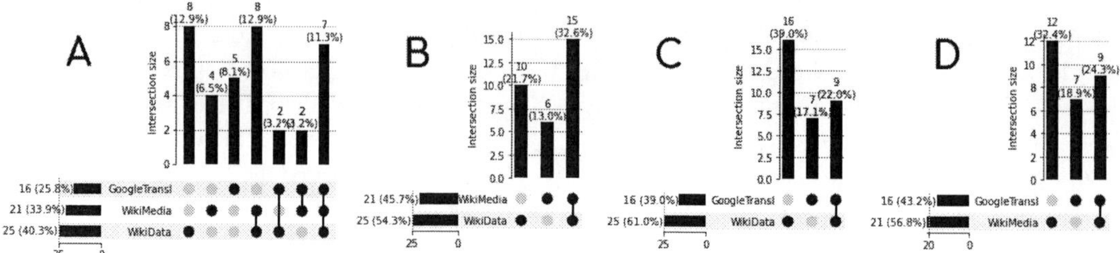

Figure 1: The leftmost columns shows the cardinality and the percentage of unique items in a given set. By unique items we mean the items that are not found in any intersection set. The remaining columns (the rightmost ones) show cardinalities and percentages of the intersection set of exactly two or three sets. A shows the unique terms in the Google Translate, the WikiMedia, and the WikiData sets (first three leftmost columns), the other four columns give information on the intersection sets of two or three sets (black dots linked by a black line). B, C, and D show in more details intersection information between exclusively two sets.

automatically translating the list of English book titles into Italian.

4.2 Evaluation and Discussion

Evaluating these three approaches is challenging, since the nature of the methods' output data is completely different, and we do not have access to a ground truth of which books match. Querying WikiData provides us entities, actual book titles. All retrieved Italian strings represent titles of Italian books that have been published and do have a corresponding English version of the book. We query the knowledge base to retrieve all entities that match with a set of conditions.

On the opposite, automatic translation and scraping the WikiMedia endpoint do not require a set of conditions to be expressed, neither allow to filter out redundant results. Scraping WikiMedia by querying English titles to retrieve the queries' corresponding Italian web page titles do include a great variety of noisy results: web pages referring to movies, theatre and semantic categories that have nothing to do with books. The automatic translation approach is even intrinsically noisier, since all strings in the list of English titles are synthetically translated, without any relationship with the actual book publication.

Due to these reasons, there is no possibility to directly evaluate and compare the accuracy of these methods. Hence we approached the evaluation indirectly, comparing the performance of the three methods on a real-scenario application. First we created a static index containing around 3400 Italian book titles by using web scraping techniques. Then we saved each matching title between each method's list of possible Italian book titles and the

index, resulting in three sets of retrieved e-books, one for each method (Google Translate, WikiData, WikiMedia). Finally, we measured, plotted and visualized information regarding the intersection size among the sets using UpSetPlot[6]. Figure 1 shows the information regarding the intersection of the WikiData, the WikiMedia, and the Google Translate sets. We can rank the methods from the most performing one to the least performing one by looking at the percentages of elements that appear exclusively in a set. By following this criterion, WikiData (12.9% of unique items) outperformed both WikiMedia (6.5% of unique items) and Google Translate (8.1% of unique items).

It is also worth noting that the methods are complementary, and that each method found at least four books not identified by any of the other methods. The relatively small amount of retrieved Italian e-books (39) might be due to the rather small size of our index of Italian e-books (around 3400), which size is a fourth of NosLivres[7] (14,845 entries)[8]. NosLivres was the index used by Kocabiyikoglu et al. (2018) for the text collection task, augmented with manual search of French e-books. They collected 315 pairs of English and French e-books.

4.3 Pre-Processing

Once we retrieved the 39 pairs of English and Italian e-books, we first extracted chapters from both the Italian and the English e-books. Secondly, we had to segment each text file (the ones resulting

---

[6]https://pypi.org/project/UpSetPlot/
[7]https://www.noslivres.net/
[8]NosLivres is updated weekly, so the exact number of entries might change

from step 1) at a sentence level granularity (without performing bitext alignment yet). To extract chapters we used *chapterize*[9], a tool that automatically splits English Gutenberg Project e-books (txt files) in chapters by using a set of regular expressions to recognize chapters headings, retrieve the text between them and finally write in a new folder a series of text files corresponding to each extracted chapter. The same approach was applied to the extracted chapters from the Italian retrieved e-books, using custom regular expressions to recognize possible Italian chapter headings.

Because great variation can be found in chapter names depending on the e-book, we had to manually check if the extracted English and Italian chapters text files really contained comparable chapters. We define comparable chapters as the ones starting and ending with paragraphs strongly semantically correlated between the English and the Italian version. It might happen that due to unseen chapter namings patterns, some chapter headings would have been missed by the regular expression, resulting in the merge of two or more chapters into one or the split of a single chapter in several text files. Therefore manual investigation of possible issues and manual troubleshooting was required to ensure the quality and the parallel property of the extracted chapters. We then stripped all leading and ending spaces from the strings and removed all newlines and tabs. Sentence segmentation was performed using two pre-trained *spaCy*[10] models (*en_core_web_sm* on the English txt files, and *it_core_news_sm* on the Italian txt files).

For our first corpus release, we focused our efforts on a pool of nine books by 8 authors, randomly selected from 39 pairs of English and Italian e-books, with a total amount of 373 pairs of comparable chapters. These 373 pairs of Italian and English texts correspond to around 130 hours of English audio aligned at a sentence granularity with their Italian textual translations and their English source texts. We thought this amount of data was meaningful enough for proceeding to the alignment experiments, prioritizing the comparison and evaluation of different alignment methods instead of using all retrieved Italian e-books (39), which would have resulted in around 500 hours of audio material to be aligned.

5 Bilingual Sentence Alignment

Kocabiyikoglu et al. (2018) only use one method for the bilingual sentence alignment task. Instead, we tested and evaluated three different methods: hunalign in conjunction with a small size hand-crafted dictionary, hunalign in conjunction with a larger bilingual dictionary automatically inferred using statistical machine translation techniques, and Vecalign (Thompson and Koehn, 2019). Vecalign is a recently proposed method to perform bilingual text alignment computing cosine similarity of embeddings of consecutive sentences. We did not experiment with Gargantua, the alignment tool used by Di Gangi et al. (2019a), mainly because the tool seems to be more effective on large documents (Abdul-Rauf et al., 2010), while we want to align each pair of English and Italian parallel chapters individually, to maintain parallelism with the English LibriVox chapter audio recordings. Hunalign is not designed for aligning documents with more than 20000 sentences, but is effective on relatively short documents (Abdul-Rauf et al., 2010), as our pairs of comparable chapters.

5.1 Hunalign with LFAligner Dictionary

textitLFAligner[11] is a bilingual sentence alignment tool built upon *hunalign*. It comes with a set of small size accurate and manually evaluated bilingual dictionaries, among which there is also an English-Italian bilingual dictionary. Kocabiyikoglu et al. (2018) used the English-French *LFAligner* dictionary as the starting material for a richer custom bilingual dictionary made of high-quality and manually annotated lexicons, resulting in a final bilingual dictionary of more than 100000 terms. We used hunalign in conjunction with the LFAligner En-It bilingual dictionary (containing around 14500 terms) as our baseline for the bilingual sentence alignment task. We set hunalign to perform two alignments. The first one uses both the lexical and the sentence-length information provided by the LFaligner dictionary and the Gale-Church algorithm. The resulting alignment is used to heuristically increase the size of the bilingual dictionary by looking at the co-occurrences found in the bi-sentences (the output of the first alignment). Finally, a second alignment is performed with the enriched bilingual dictionary (resulting from the first alignment).

[9]https://github.com/JonathanReeve/chapterize
[10]https://spacy.io/

[11]https://sourceforge.net/projects/aligner/

5.2 Hunalign with a Bilingual Dictionary Inferred with Moses and Giza++

Since the size of the *LFAligner* Italian-English dictionary was rather small (around 14500 terms) and we did not find other accurate and manually annotated freely available English-Italian lexicons, we investigated if a large automatically created lexicon could be useful. We compiled a large English-Italian corpus (containing 3131200 parallel sentences) by concatenating the *Europarl* (Koehn, 2005), the *Wikipedia* (Wołk and Marasek, 2014), the *GlobalVoices*[12], and the *books*[13] corpora from *OPUS* (Tiedemann, 2012). We used *Giza++* (Och and Ney, 2003) to align the corpus, followed by using Moses SMT (Koehn et al., 2007) to symmetrize the directional alignments, and extract a lexical translation table. The bidirectional tables contain a great amount of extremely low-probability translation terms hypotheses. We inferred a bilingual dictionary containing 692437 bilingual terms by filtering out the terms scoring less than 0.10. This inferred lexicon was used with Hunalign.

5.3 Vecalign

Rather than relying on sentence-length information and bilingual dictionaries, the sentences to be aligned are mapped into their vector representations and the alignment is done by computing the cosine similarity of the sentence embeddings. The underlying theoretical principle is that sentence embeddings seem to capture semantic information. Therefore, the higher the cosine similarity, the higher the probability two sentences in different languages have the same meaning. Vecalign requires multilingual embeddings of consecutive sentences. By concatenation of consecutive sentences we mean all combination of consecutive sentences in a window of size N. If there is a document containing the 3 sentences: *"Hi.", "I'm Jack.", "Nice to meet you."* and the window size is equal to 3 all possible consecutive sentences would be the original three sentences *"Hi.", "I'm Jack.", "Nice to meet you.", Hi. I'm Jack", "I'm Jack. Nice to meet you.", "Hi. I'm Jack. Nice to meet you.".* By embedding consecutive sentences, Vecalign work in scenarios where one sentence in language A should be aligned with multiple sentences in language B (e.g. Italian: "Ciao, sono Jack" - gloss "Hi, I am

Jack" - English: "Hi.", "I am Jack") or viceversa. We used Facebook LASER (Schwenk and Douze, 2017; Schwenk and Li, 2018; Schwenk, 2018) to map into vectors all possible English and Italian consecutive sentences in a window of size 10 for each pair of documents to be aligned.

5.4 Evaluation Methodology

There are two main challenges in evaluating the sentence aligners. First, the lack of a gold standard file for computing the F1 score. Second, the fact that in many cases sentence alignments are not ambiguous and are easy to spot. For instance, Varga et al. (2007) reports precision and recall of over 0.97 on several texts. Lacking a gold standard, we have to resort to evaluating a small sample manually. If we sample sentences randomly, there will probably be very little difference between the aligners, due to the high number of easy-to-align sentences. Instead, we decided to focus our evaluation effort on a set of difficult alignment scenarios. Therefore, we focused only on the cases in which the results of the three aligners differed: a subset of 2030 likely difficult alignments from all pairs of 373 aligned chapters, with a total of 70204 possible alignments.[14] We then sampled 200 cases from this pool. For each sentence we compared the results of the three methods by assigning three possible values: correct alignment, wrong alignment, or partial alignment. By correct alignment we mean a perfect one to one, one to many, or many to one alignment: e.g. the English sentence *"It was delightful once upon a time"* aligned with the Italian sentence *"Era un piacere allora!"*. By wrong alignment we mean the cases in which the alignment was totally wrong: e.g. the English sentence *'Yours affectionately'* aligned with the Italian sentence *'Barkis ha intenzione di andare'* (gloss:*'Barkis plans to go'*). Finally, by partial alignment we mean the cases in which the alignment was neither totally wrong, nor totally correct, but only partially correct. This usually happens when a different number of sentences is used in the two texts to express the same meaning: e.g. the English sentence *'I see it now'* is aligned with the Italian sentence *'Mi sembra di rivederla: una lunga sala, con tre lunghe file di*

---

[14]The number of overlapping alignments between the systems could give an idea of the overall performance of the sentence aligners. While not all identical alignments can be expected to be correct, a high proportion of them are likely to be. Hunalign with and without the inferred dictionary have a 93.6% agreement. Hunalign and Vecalign have a 79.2% agreement if we exclude zero alignments not given by Hunalign.

	Hunalign	Hunalign+Inf	Vecalign
Correct	42	43	169
Wrong	108	89	5
Partial	50	68	26

Table 1: Evaluation of the bilingual text alignment task. For each method the number of correct, wrong, and partial alignments is given out of a selected pool of 200 sentences. *Inf* stands for the inferred dictionary.

piccoli scrittoi' (gloss: *I see it now. A long room with three long rows of desks'*).

5.5 Results and Discussion

Table 1 shows the results of the comparison of the 200 aligned sentences. For each one of them, we compared the alignments provided by our baseline, hunalign in conjunction with the inferred dictionary, and Vecalign. Vecalign outperforms the two variants of hunalign on this sample, with 169 correct alignments and only 5 wrong alignments, compared to hunalign which had just over 40 correct alignments for either variant. We explain the outperformance of *Vecalign* over the two hunalign methods to be strictly correlated to the use of multilingual embeddings of possible consecutive sentences. Computing the cosine similarity of consecutive sentences embeddings allows an easier spot of one to many, or many to one alignments. For instance, Vecalign managed to align correctly the two English sentences *'I see it now.'* and *'A long room with three long rows of desks.* with the single Italian sentence: *'Mi sembra di rivederla: una lunga sala, con tre lunghe file di piccoli scrittoi'* (gloss: *I see it now. A long room with three long rows of desks'*). Furthermore, *Vecalign* also gave as output a zero to one or zero to many alignments, which might mean that it filtered out the cases where the two e-books differed drastically in terms of paragraphs and sentences. For these reasons, we decided to use Vecalign for the final corpus. Approaching the sentence alignment problem using sentence embeddings has the advantage of obliterating bilingual lexical resources. The results of the two hunalign methods gives interesting insights over the quality and the size of the bilingual dictionary supporting the Gale-Church alignment algorithm. The use of the inferred dictionary (roughly six times the size of the manually annotated dictionary) led to a reduction of the amount of wrong alignments (19 less errors), without increasing the amount of the correct alignments.

Correct	Mild Errors	Severe Error
204	2	4

Table 2: Evaluation table for the forced alignment task with *Aeneas*

6 Forced Alignment

Forced alignment is the process to return time intervals matching word or sentence utterances in a audio file with their corresponding strings in a parallel text file. We forced the alignment between 373 LibriVox wav files and the English side of our textual parallel corpus, using Aeneas[15] rather than Gentle (as in Kocabiyikoglu et al. (2018)).

6.1 Gentle and Aeneas

Both tools are used for forcing speech to text alignment, but they differ in the way forced alignment is reached. Gentle is based on a pre-trained Kaldi (Povey et al., 2011) English ASR model: a hidden Markov model (HMM) determines the location of phonemes and words in the audio. For this reason, Gentle returns the time intervals for each word. Sentence time intervals can be obtained by a post-processing step on the Gentle output. The advantage of this method is that it can handle large portions of spurious text or audio. Aeneas is based on a TTS-DTW (text-to-speech and dynamic time warping) algorithm: the text transcript is first read by a text-to-speech software, then the dynamic time warping algorithm (Sakoe and Chiba, 1978) is deployed to compare the two audio sequences and return a synchronisation map with time intervals. The advantage of this approach is that it directly gives the sentence time intervals. The disadvantage is that it cannot handle large portions of spurious text: the audio has to match the text. As we did not encounter large portions of spurious text and audio in our corpus[16], we chose to use Aeneas for the forced alignment task.

6.2 Evaluation

We sampled 210 pairs of audio segments and their corresponding English texts. Manual evaluation was carried out by listening to each audio segment while reading its corresponding text file. Each

---

[15] https://github.com/readbeyond/aeneas

[16] the only discrepancies between the 373 LibriVox chapter audio recordings and our corpus were the LibriVox disclaimers at the beginning or at the end of each LibriVox recording, which we manually cut

	Number		Avg
Speakers	98		
Hours	131.23		
Chapters	373	**Per Speaker**	3.80
Segments	60561	**Duration**	7.80 s

Table 3: Corpus statistics, including the total number of chapters, speakers, segments and hours (rounded to decimals). In addition, the average (Avg) segment duration and the average number of chapters read by each speaker is given

audio-to-text alignment was given one of the following labels: *correct*, *mild*, and *severe*. The label *correct* indicates that text and audio match and all words are pronounced entirely and clearly, without brutal and abrupt cuts. The label *mild error* describes a scenario where a letter was missing from the starting or ending of the audio or was not clearly pronounced. The *severe error* label indicates that the audio and its corresponding text are severely off-sync or completely wrong. Due to the fact that *severe errors* can cause error propagation, every time we ran across a severe error, we also checked the preceding and following audio-to-text alignments. Table 2 shows the results of our manual evaluation. Out of 210 manually checked alignments, we encountered only 4 severe errors and none of them caused error propagation. The few severe errors were due to actual mismatches between the audio and the text (e.g. the speaker decided to read a footnote from the original e-book).

7 Corpus Statistics and Structure

IESTAC[17] contains 60561 triplets of English audio, English source text, and Italian textual translation. Statistics are given in Table 3. The corpus is available as a zipped folder containing two parallel raw text files[18] and nine folders, one for each book. Each folder is named after a Gutenberg Project Ebook ID. Each one of these folders contains several sub-folders, one for each aligned chapter. The chapter folders are named as increasing integers. In each chapter folder, there are several triplets of files. The alignment is preserved by the base-name notation: each element of the triplet has a base-name composed of three concatenated integers (E-bookID, ChapterID, SegmentID). The file-

name extension is used to disambiguate between the audio, the Italian textual translation, and the English source text (e.g. 83_07_33.wav, 83_07_33.it, 83_07_33.en). We also provide the users with a SQL database to allow them to query the corpus according to their needs.

8 Future Work

In future work, we want first of all to perform an extrinsic evaluation of our corpus on both automatic speech recognition and end-to-end speech-to-text machine translation tasks. A possible tool for that might be FBK-Fairseq-ST[19]. We also want to further improve the quality of the alignments by filtering out low-quality ones. For such task we might investigate the use of alignment scores, character error rate, language model perplexity, sentence embeddings similarity scores, and length ratio heuristic. Another direction of interest is to work towards a full taxonomy for collecting speech-to-text datasets for machine translation.

9 Conclusion

We have explored methods for creating a bilingual corpus with English speech and text, and Italian text. The corpus collection is based on available English speech and text in the LibriVox and the Project Gutenberg collection of audiobooks and e-books, which we mapped to Italian texts in this work. We explored and evaluated a number of methods for the different steps needed in the corpus creation, which might guide future work in creating corpora for other language pairs. For the text collection, we needed to map English books to their equivalent Italian translations. We proposed three methods based on WikiData matching, Wikipedia matching, and MT of book titles. We found that the three methods were complementary, each contributing some unique titles. The next step was bilingual sentence alignment, for which we found that Vecalign, a method based on computing the cosine similarity of consecutive sentence embeddings, outperformed the traditional Gale-Church method when dealing with difficult alignments. Finally we argued for the use of a TTS dynamic time warping system for forcing the alignment between English speech and text, and showed that the results were of high quality. As part of this work we release IESTAC

---

[17]`https://github.com/`
`Giuseppe-Della-Corte/IESTAC`

[18]*parallel.it* and *parallel.en* contain respectively: total tokens (1425072 - 1577118), unique tokens (63,774 - 38,325)

[19]`https://github.com/mattiadg/`
`FBK-Fairseq-ST`

References

Sadaf Abdul-Rauf, Mark Fishel, Patrik Lambert, Sandra Noubours, and Rico Sennrich. 2010. Evaluation of sentence alignment systems. Technical report, Fifth MT Marathon.

Antonios Anastasopoulos and David Chiang. 2018. Tied multitask learning for neural speech translation. In *Proceedings of the 2018 Conference of the North American Chapter of the Association for Computational Linguistics: Human Language Technologies, Volume 1 (Long Papers)*, pages 82–91, New Orleans, Louisiana. Association for Computational Linguistics.

Rosana Ardila, Megan Branson, Kelly Davis, Michael Kohler, Josh Meyer, Michael Henretty, Reuben Morais, Lindsay Saunders, Francis Tyers, and Gregor Weber. 2020. Common voice: A massively-multilingual speech corpus. In *Proceedings of the 12th Language Resources and Evaluation Conference*, pages 4218–4222, Marseille, France. European Language Resources Association.

Sören Auer, Christian Bizer, Georgi Kobilarov, Jens Lehmann, Richard Cyganiak, and Zachary Ives. 2007. Dbpedia: A nucleus for a web of open data. In *ISWC 2007, ASWC 2007: The semantic web*, Lecture Notes in Computer Science, vol 4825, pages 722–735. Springer, Busan, Korea.

Benjamin Beilharz, Xin Sun, Sariya Karimova, and Stefan Riezler. 2020. LibriVoxDeEn: A corpus for German-to-English speech translation and German speech recognition. In *Proceedings of the 12th Language Resources and Evaluation Conference*, pages 3590–3594, Marseille, France. European Language Resources Association.

Alexandre Bérard, Laurent Besacier, Ali Can Kocabiyikoglu, and Olivier Pietquin. 2018. End-to-end automatic speech translation of audiobooks. In *2018 IEEE International Conference on Acoustics, Speech and Signal Processing (ICASSP)*, pages 6224–6228, Calgary, Canada. IEEE.

Alexandre Bérard, Olivier Pietquin, Christophe Servan, and Laurent Besacier. 2016. Listen and translate: A proof of concept for end-to-end speech-to-text translation. In *NIPS Workshop on end-to-end learning for speech and audio processing*, Barcelona, Spain.

Alan W Black. 2019. CMU wilderness multilingual speech dataset. In *ICASSP 2019-2019 IEEE International Conference on Acoustics, Speech and Signal Processing (ICASSP)*, pages 5971–5975, Brighton, UK. IEEE.

Fabienne Braune and Alexander Fraser. 2010. Improved unsupervised sentence alignment for symmetrical and asymmetrical parallel corpora. In *Coling 2010: Posters*, pages 81–89, Beijing, China. Coling 2010 Organizing Committee.

Giuseppe Della Corte. 2020. Text and Speech Alignment Methods for Speech Translation Corpora Creation: Augmenting English LibriVox Recordings with Italian Textual Translations. Master's thesis, Uppsala University, Sweden.

Mattia A. Di Gangi, Roldano Cattoni, Luisa Bentivogli, Matteo Negri, and Marco Turchi. 2019a. MuST-C: a Multilingual Speech Translation Corpus. In *Proceedings of the 2019 Conference of the North American Chapter of the Association for Computational Linguistics: Human Language Technologies, Volume 1 (Long and Short Papers)*, pages 2012–2017, Minneapolis, Minnesota. Association for Computational Linguistics.

Mattia Antonino Di Gangi, Matteo Negri, Roldano Cattoni, Dessi Roberto, and Marco Turchi. 2019b. Enhancing transformer for end-to-end speech-to-text translation. In *Machine Translation Summit XVII*, pages 21–31, Dublin, Ireland.

Pierre Godard, Gilles Adda, Martine Adda-Decker, Juan Benjumea, Laurent Besacier, Jamison Cooper-Leavitt, Guy-Noel Kouarata, Lori Lamel, Hélène Maynard, Markus Mueller, Annie Rialland, Sebastian Stueker, François Yvon, and Marcely Zanon-Boito. 2018. A very low resource language speech corpus for computational language documentation experiments. In *Proceedings of the Eleventh International Conference on Language Resources and Evaluation (LREC 2018)*, Miyazaki, Japan. European Language Resources Association (ELRA).

Javier Iranzo-Sánchez, Joan Albert Silvestre-Cerdà, Javier Jorge, Nahuel Roselló, Adrià Giménez, Albert Sanchis, Jorge Civera, and Alfons Juan. 2020. Europarl-ST: A multilingual corpus for speech translation of parliamentary debates. In *ICASSP 2020-2020 IEEE International Conference on Acoustics, Speech and Signal Processing (ICASSP)*, pages 8229–8233, Barcelona, Spain. IEEE.

Jodi Kearns. 2014. Librivox: Free public domain audiobooks. *Reference Reviews*, 28(1):7–8.

Ali Can Kocabiyikoglu, Laurent Besacier, and Olivier Kraif. 2018. Augmenting librispeech with French translations: A multimodal corpus for direct speech translation evaluation. In *Proceedings of the Eleventh International Conference on Language Resources and Evaluation (LREC 2018)*, Miyazaki, Japan. European Language Resources Association (ELRA).

Philipp Koehn. 2005. Europarl: A parallel corpus for statistical machine translation. In *Machine Translation Summit X*, volume 5, pages 79–86, Phuket, Thailand.

Philipp Koehn, Hieu Hoang, Alexandra Birch, Chris Callison-Burch, Marcello Federico, Nicola Bertoldi, Brooke Cowan, Wade Shen, Christine Moran, Richard Zens, Chris Dyer, Ondřej Bojar, Alexandra Constantin, and Evan Herbst. 2007. Moses: Open source toolkit for statistical machine translation. In *Proceedings of the 45th Annual Meeting of the Association for Computational Linguistics Companion Volume Proceedings of the Demo and Poster Sessions*, pages 177–180, Prague, Czech Republic. Association for Computational Linguistics.

Franz Josef Och and Hermann Ney. 2003. A systematic comparison of various statistical alignment models. *Computational Linguistics*, 29(1):19–51.

Vassil Panayotov, Guoguo Chen, Daniel Povey, and Sanjeev Khudanpur. 2015. Librispeech: an ASR corpus based on public domain audio books. In *2015 IEEE International Conference on Acoustics, Speech and Signal Processing (ICASSP)*, pages 5206–5210, Brisbane, Australia. IEEE.

Daniel Povey, Arnab Ghoshal, Gilles Boulianne, Lukas Burget, Ondrej Glembek, Nagendra Goel, Mirko Hannemann, Petr Motlicek, Yanmin Qian, Petr Schwarz, Jan Silovsky, Georg Stemmer, and Karel Vesely. 2011. The Kaldi speech recognition toolkit. In *IEEE 2011 workshop on automatic speech recognition and understanding*, location = Hilton Waikoloa Village, Hawaii, US,. IEEE Signal Processing Society.

Nicholas Ruiz, Mattia Antonino Di Gangi, Nicola Bertoldi, and Marcello Federico. 2017. Assessing the tolerance of neural machine translation systems against speech recognition errors. In *Proceedings of Interspeech 2017*, page 2635–2639, Stockholm, Sweden.

Hiroaki Sakoe and Seibi Chiba. 1978. Dynamic programming algorithm optimization for spoken word recognition. *IEEE transactions on acoustics, speech, and signal processing*, 26(1):43–49.

Ramon Sanabria, Ozan Caglayan, Shruti Palaskar, Desmond Elliott, Loïc Barrault, Lucia Specia, and Florian Metze. 2018. How2: a large-scale dataset for multimodal language understanding. In *Visually Grounded Interaction and Language (ViGIL), NeurIPS 2018 Workshop*, Montreal, Canada.

Holger Schwenk. 2018. Filtering and mining parallel data in a joint multilingual space. In *Proceedings of the 56th Annual Meeting of the Association for Computational Linguistics (Volume 2: Short Papers)*, pages 228–234, Melbourne, Australia. Association for Computational Linguistics.

Holger Schwenk and Matthijs Douze. 2017. Learning joint multilingual sentence representations with neural machine translation. In *Proceedings of the 2nd Workshop on Representation Learning for NLP*, pages 157–167, Vancouver, Canada. Association for Computational Linguistics.

Holger Schwenk and Xian Li. 2018. A corpus for multilingual document classification in eight languages. In *Proceedings of the Eleventh International Conference on Language Resources and Evaluation (LREC 2018)*, Miyazaki, Japan. European Language Resources Association (ELRA).

Bryan Stroube. 2003. Literary freedom: Project Gutenberg. *XRDS: Crossroads, The ACM Magazine for Students*, 10(1).

Brian Thompson and Philipp Koehn. 2019. Vecalign: Improved sentence alignment in linear time and space. In *Proceedings of the 2019 Conference on Empirical Methods in Natural Language Processing and the 9th International Joint Conference on Natural Language Processing (EMNLP-IJCNLP)*, pages 1342–1348, Hong Kong, China. Association for Computational Linguistics.

Jörg Tiedemann. 2012. Parallel data, tools and interfaces in OPUS. In *Proceedings of the Eighth International Conference on Language Resources and Evaluation (LREC'12)*, pages 2214–2218, Istanbul, Turkey. European Language Resources Association (ELRA).

Astrid Van Aggelen, Laura Hollink, Max Kemman, Martijn Kleppe, and Henri Beunders. 2017. The debates of the European parliament as linked open data. *Semantic Web*, 8(2):271–281.

Dániel Varga, Péter Halácsy, András Kornai, Viktor Nagy, László Németh, and Viktor Trón. 2007. Parallel corpora for medium density languages. In *Recent Advances in Natural Language Processing (RANLP)*, pages 247–258, Borovets, Bulgaria.

Denny Vrandečić and Markus Krötzsch. 2014. Wikidata: a free collaborative knowledgebase. *Communications of the ACM*, 57(10):78–85.

Changhan Wang, Juan Pino, Anne Wu, and Jiatao Gu. 2020a. CoVoST: A diverse multilingual speech-to-text translation corpus. In *Proceedings of The 12th Language Resources and Evaluation Conference*, pages 4197–4203, Marseille, France. European Language Resources Association.

Changhan Wang, Anne Wu, and Juan Pino. 2020b. CoVoST 2 and massively multilingual speech-to-text translation. *arXiv e-prints arXiv:2007.10310v2*.

Ron J Weiss, Jan Chorowski, Navdeep Jaitly, Yonghui Wu, and Zhifeng Chen. 2017. Sequence-to-sequence models can directly translate foreign speech. In *Proceedings of Interspeech 2017*, pages 2625–2629, Stockholm, Sweden.

Krzysztof Wołk and Krzysztof Marasek. 2014. Building subject-aligned comparable corpora and mining it for truly parallel sentence pairs. *Procedia Technology*, 18:126–132.

Unsupervised Keyword Extraction for Full-Sentence VQA

Kohei Uehara
The University of Tokyo
uehara@mi.t.u-tokyo.ac.jp

Tatsuya Harada
The University of Tokyo
RIKEN
harada@mi.t.u-tokyo.ac.jp

Abstract

In the majority of the existing Visual Question Answering (VQA) research, the answers consist of short, often single words, as per instructions given to the annotators during dataset construction. This study envisions a VQA task for natural situations, where the answers are more likely to be sentences rather than single words. To bridge the gap between this natural VQA and existing VQA approaches, a novel unsupervised keyword extraction method is proposed. The method is based on the principle that the full-sentence answers can be decomposed into two parts: one that contains new information answering the question (i.e., keywords), and one that contains information already included in the question. Discriminative decoders were designed to achieve such decomposition, and the method was experimentally implemented on VQA datasets containing full-sentence answers. The results show that the proposed model can accurately extract the keywords without being given explicit annotations describing them.

1 Introduction

Visual recognition is one of the most actively researched fields; this research is expected to be applied to real-world systems such as robots. Since innumerable object classes exist in the real world, training all of them in advance is impossible. Thus, to train image recognition models, it is important for real-world intelligent systems to actively acquire information. One promising approach to acquire information on the fly is *learning by asking*, i.e., generating questions to humans about unknown objects, and consequently learning new knowledge from the human response (Misra et al., 2018; Uehara et al., 2018; Shen et al., 2019). This implies that if we can build a Visual Question Answering (VQA) system (Antol et al., 2015) that functions in the real

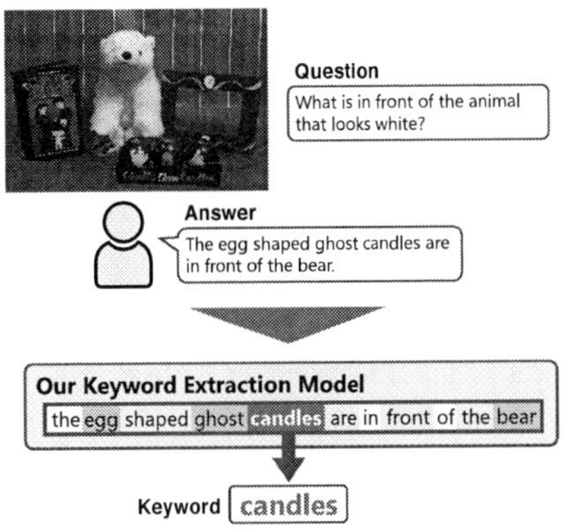

Figure 1: Example of the proposed task – keyword extraction from full-sentence VQA. Given an image, the question, and the full-sentence answer, the keyword extraction model extracts a keyword from the full-sentence answer. In this example, the word "candles" is the most important part, answering the question "What is in front of the animal that looks white?". Therefore, "candles" is considered as the keyword of the answer.

world and extracts knowledge from human responses, we can realize an intelligent system that can learn autonomously.

VQA is a well-known vision and language task which aims to develop a system that can answer a question about an image. One typical dataset used in VQA is the VQA v2 dataset (Goyal et al., 2017). The answers in the VQA v2 dataset are essentially single words. This is because the annotators are instructed to keep the answer as short as possible when constructing the dataset.

The ultimate goal of the present work is to gain knowledge through VQA that can be easily transferred to other tasks, such as object class recognition and object detection. Therefore, the knowledge (VQA answers) should be represented by a single word, such as a class label. However, in real-world dialog, answers are rarely ex-

51

Proceedings of the First International Workshop on Natural Language Processing Beyond Text, pages 51–59
Online, November 20, 2020. ©2020 Association for Computational Linguistics

pressed by single words; rather, they are often expressed as complete sentences. In fact, in VisDial v1.0 (Das et al., 2017), a dataset of natural conversations about images that does not have a word limit for answers, the average length of answers is 6.5 words. This is significantly longer than the average length of the answers in the VQA v2 dataset (1.2 words).

To bridge the gap between existing VQA research and real-world VQA, a challenging problem must be solved: identifying the word in the sentence that corresponds to the answer to the question. It must also be considered that full-sentence answers provided by humans are likely to follow a variety of sentence structures. Thus, the traditional approaches, such as rule-based approaches based on Part-of-Speech tagging or shallow parsing, require a great deal of work on defining rules in order to extract the keywords. Our key challenge is to propose a novel keyword extraction method that leverages information from images and questions as clues, without the heavy work of annotating keywords or defining the rules.

This work handles the task of extracting a keyword when a full-sentence answer is obtained from VQA (**Full-sentence VQA**). The simplest approach to this task is to construct a dataset containing full-sentence answers and keyword annotations, and then train a model based on this dataset in a supervised manner. However, the cost of constructing a VQA dataset with full-sentence answers and keyword annotations is very high. If a keyword extraction model can be trained on a dataset without keyword annotations, we can eliminate the high cost of collecting keyword annotations.

We propose an unsupervised keyword extraction model using a full-sentence VQA dataset which contains no keyword annotations. Here, the principle is based on the intuition that the keyword is the most informative word in the full-sentence answer, and contains the information that is not included in the question (i.e., the concise answer). Essentially, the full-sentence answer can be decomposed into two types of words: (1) the keyword information that is not included in the question, and (2) the information that is already included in the question. For example, in the answer "The egg shaped ghost candles are in front of the bear." to the question "What is in front of the animal that looks white?", the word "candles"

is the keyword, while the remaining part "The egg shaped ghost *something* is in front of the bear" is either information already included in the question or additional information about the keyword. In this case, words like "egg," "ghost," and "bear" are also not in the question, making it difficult to find the keyword via naive methods, e.g., rule-based keyword extraction. Our proposed model utilizes image features and question features to calculate the importance score for each word in the full-sentence answer. Therefore, based on the contents of the image and the question, the model can accurately estimate which words in the full-sentence answer are important. To the best of our knowledge, this is the first attempt at extracting a keyword from full-sentence VQA in an unsupervised manner. The main contributions of this work are as follows: (1) We propose a novel task of extracting keywords from full-sentence VQA with no keyword annotations. (2) We designed a novel, unsupervised keyword extraction model by decomposing the full-sentence answer. (3) We conducted experiments on two VQA datasets, and provided both qualitative and quantitative results that show the effectiveness of our model.

2 Related Work

2.1 Unsupervised Keyword Extraction for Text

Unsupervised keyword extraction methods can be broadly classified into two categories: graph-based methods and statistical methods.

Graph-based methods construct graphs from target documents by using co-occurrence between words (Mihalcea and Tarau, 2004; Wan and Xiao). These methods are only applicable to documents with a certain length, as they require the words in the document to co-occur multiple times. The target document in this work is a full-sentence answer of VQA, whose average length is about 10 words. Therefore, graph-based methods are not suitable here.

Statistical methods rely on statistics obtained from a document. The most basic statistical method is TF-IDF (Ramos, 2003), which calculates the term frequency and inverse document frequency and scores each word in the target document. Recent work such as EmbedRank (Bennani-Smires et al., 2018) have utilized word embeddings for the unsupervised keyword extraction. EmbedRank calculates the cosine similarity

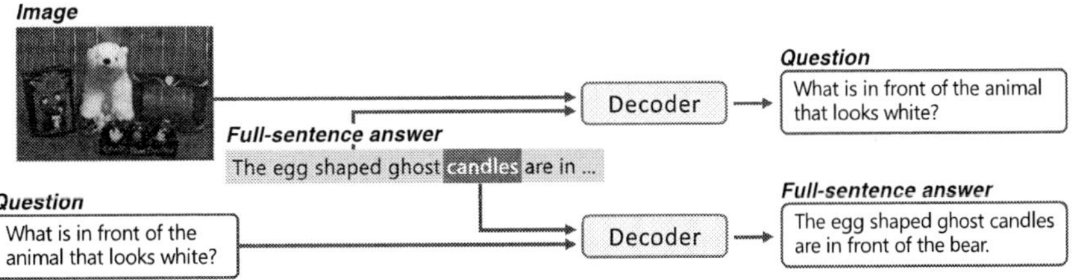

Figure 2: Illustration of the key concept. In this example, the word "candles" is the keyword for the full-sentence answer, "The egg shaped ghost candles are in front of the bear." We consider the keyword extraction task as the decomposition of the full-sentence answer into answer information and question information. Therefore, if the keyword (i.e., the most informative word in the full-sentence answer) can be accurately extracted, the original full-sentence answer can be reconstructed from it. Additionally, the question can be reconstructed from the decomposed question information in the full-sentence answer.

between the candidate word (or phrase) embeddings and the sentence embeddings to retrieve the most representative word of the text.

2.2 Visual Question Answering

VQA is a well-known task that involves learning from image-related questions and answers. The most popular VQA dataset is VQA v2 (Goyal et al., 2017), and much research has used this dataset for performance evaluations. In VQA v2, the average number of words in an answer is only 1.2, and the variety of answers is relatively limited.

As stated in Section 1, in natural question answering by humans, the answers will be expressed as a sentence rather than a single word. Some datasets that have both full-sentence answers and keyword annotations exist.

FSVQA (Shin et al., 2016) is a VQA dataset with answers in the form of full sentences. In it, full-sentence answers are automatically generated by applying the numerous rule-based natural language processing patterns to the questions and single-word answers in the VQA v1 dataset (Antol et al., 2015).

The recently proposed dataset, named GQA (Hudson and Manning, 2019), also contains automatically generated full-sentence answers. This dataset is constructed on the Visual Genome (Krishna et al., 2017), which has rich and complex annotations about images, including dense captions, questions, and scene graphs. The questions and answers (both single-word and full-sentence) in the GQA dataset are created from scene graph annotations of the images.

The full-sentence answers in both datasets described above are annotated automatically, i.e.,

not by humans. Therefore, neither dataset has both full-sentence answers and manually annotated keywords.

2.3 Attention

The attention mechanism is a technique originally proposed in machine translation (Bahdanau et al., 2015), aimed at focusing on the most important part of the input sequences for a task. Since the method proposed herein utilizes an attention mechanism to calculate the importance score of the word in the full-sentence answer, some prior works on attention mechanisms are discussed.

In general, an attention mechanism essentially learns the mapping between a query and key-value pairs. Transformer (Vaswani et al., 2017) is one of the most popular attention mechanisms for machine translation. It enables machine translation without using recurrent neural networks, using a self-attention mechanism and feed-forward networks instead.

Another study uses an attention mechanism for weakly supervised keyword extraction (Wu et al., 2018). They first trained a model for document classification and extracted the word to which the model pays "attention" to perform the classification. This system requires additional annotations of document class labels to train the model, whereas we aim to extract keywords without any additional annotations.

3 Model

This section describes the proposed method in detail.

First, the principal concept of the model is shown in Figure 2. To extract the keyword, we intend to obtain two features from the full-sentence answer, each representing the keyword information and the information derived from the question, respectively. To ensure that these two features discriminatively include keyword information and question information, we intend to reconstruct the original questions and answers from the question features and keyword features, respectively. Thus, if we successfully extract the keyword and the question information from the full-sentence answer, we can reconstruct original full-sentence answer and the question. Essentially, given an image, its corresponding question, and full-sentence answer, our proposed model extracts the keyword of the answer by decomposing the keyword information and the question information in the answer.

3.1 Overview

An overview of the model is shown in Figure 3. To realize decomposition-based keyword extraction, we designed a model which consists of the encoder $\mathbf{E}$, the attention scoring modules $\mathbf{S}_a$ and $\mathbf{S}_q$, and the decoder modules $\mathbf{D}_{all}$, $\mathbf{D}_a$, and $\mathbf{D}_q$.

An image I and the corresponding question Q and full-sentence answer $A = \{w_1^{(a)}, w_2^{(a)}, \ldots, w_n^{(a)}\}$ are considered as the model input. Here, $w_i^{(a)}$ represents the i-th word in the full-sentence answer.

Given I and Q, $\mathbf{E}$ extracts image and question features and integrates them into joint features f_j, i.e., $\mathbf{E}(I, Q) = f_j$.

Next, $\mathbf{S}_a$ and $\mathbf{S}_q$ use f_j and A as input and output the weight vectors a_k and a_q. Here, $a_k = \{a_1^{(k)}, a_2^{(k)}, \ldots, a_n^{(k)}\}$ and $a_q = \{a_1^{(q)}, a_2^{(q)}, \ldots, a_n^{(q)}\}$ for each word in A. We denote $a_i \in (0, 1)$ as the weight score of the i-th word in A.

Then, we consider the keyword vector f_k as the embedding vector of the word with the highest weight score in a_k. Meanwhile, the question information vector f_q is considered as the weighted sum of the embedding vectors of A corresponding to the weight score a_q.

Following this, $\mathbf{D}_{all}$ uses LSTM to reconstruct the original full-sentence answer using f_q and f_k. f_q and f_k are intended to represent the question information and the keyword vector of the full-sentence answer, respectively. However, $\mathbf{D}_{all}$ only ensures that both features have the information of the full-sentence answer. To separate them, we designed the additional decoders, $\mathbf{D}_a$ and $\mathbf{D}_q$. The former reconstructs the BoW features of the answer using f_k, while the latter reconstructs those of the question using f_q with auxiliary vectors. The objective of this operation is to make f_k and f_q representative features for the full-sentence answer and the question, respectively.

The entire model is trained to minimize the disparity between the reconstructed sentences A_{recon} and the original full-sentence answers, as well as that between the BoW features of the full-sentence answers and the questions.

3.2 Encoder

The module $\mathbf{E}$ encodes the image I and the question Q and obtains the image feature f_I, the question feature f_Q, and the joint feature f_j. To generate f_I, we use the image feature extracted from a deep CNN, which is pre-trained on a large-scale image recognition dataset. For f_Q, each word token was converted into a word embeddings and averaged. Following this, l_2 normalization was performed on both features. Finally, those features were concatenated to the joint feature $f_j \in \mathbb{R}^{d_j}$, i.e., $\mathbf{E}(I, Q) = f_j = [f_I; f_Q]$, where d_j is the dimension of the joint feature and $[;]$ indicates concatenation. Note that we did not update the model parameters of $\mathbf{E}$ during training.

3.3 Attention Scoring Module

This module takes f_j as input and weights each words in the full-sentence answer. We used two of these modules, $\mathbf{S}_a$ and $\mathbf{S}_q$. $\mathbf{S}_a$ and $\mathbf{S}_q$ compute the weights based on the importance of a word for the full-sentence answer and that for the question, respectively. $\mathbf{S}_a$ and $\mathbf{S}_q$ have a nearly identical structure. Therefore, the details of $\mathbf{S}_a$ are presented first, following which the difference between $\mathbf{S}_a$ and $\mathbf{S}_q$ is described.

The weight scoring in these modules is based on the attention mechanism used in Transformer (Vaswani et al., 2017). First, each word in the full-sentence answer was encoded, and the full-sentence answer vector $f_A = \{w_1^{(a)}, w_2^{(a)}, \ldots, w_n^{(a)}\} \in \mathbb{R}^{d_e \times n}$ was created. Here, $w_i^{(a)}$ denotes the embedding vector of the i-th word, n is the length of the full-sentence answer, and d_e is the dimension of the word embedding vector. To represent the word order, positional encoding was applied to f_A. Specifically, before feeding f_A into scoring modules, we add positional embedding vectors to f_A, similar to

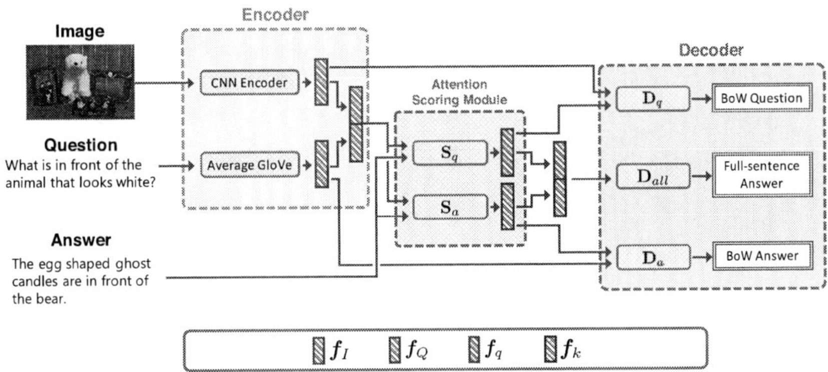

Figure 3: Overall pipeline of the model. First, the Encoder Module extracts the image features $\boldsymbol{f}_I$ and the question features $\boldsymbol{f}_Q$ and integrates them into a joint feature $\boldsymbol{f}_j$. Then, the Attention Scoring Modules $\mathbf{S}_a$ and $\mathbf{S}_q$ compute the attention weight and calculate the weighted sum of the word-embedding vectors of the full-sentence answer. The output of $\mathbf{S}_a$ i.e., $\boldsymbol{f}_k$, is the keyword-aware feature of the full-sentence answer, and the output of $\mathbf{S}_q$ i.e., $\boldsymbol{f}_q$, is the question-aware feature. $\mathbf{D}_{all}$ reconstructs the full-sentence answer from both $\boldsymbol{f}_k$ and $\boldsymbol{f}_q$. $\mathbf{D}_a$ estimates the Bag-of-Words(BoW) feature of the full-sentence answer from $\boldsymbol{f}_k$ and $\boldsymbol{f}_Q$. Additionally, $\mathbf{D}_q$ estimates the BoW feature of the question from $\boldsymbol{f}_q$ and $\boldsymbol{f}_I$.

those introduced in BERT (Devlin et al., 2019).

We describe our attention mechanism as a mapping between Query and Key-Value pairs. First, we calculate Query vector $\boldsymbol{Q} \in \mathbb{R}^h$, Key vector $\boldsymbol{K} \in \mathbb{R}^{h \times n}$, and Value vector $\boldsymbol{V} \in \mathbb{R}^{h \times n}$.

$$\boldsymbol{Q} = \text{FFN}_q(\boldsymbol{f}_j) \tag{1}$$

$$\boldsymbol{K} = \text{FFN}_k(\boldsymbol{f}_A) \tag{2}$$

$$\boldsymbol{V} = \text{FFN}_v(\boldsymbol{f}_A) = \{\boldsymbol{v}_1^{(a)}, \boldsymbol{v}_2^{(a)}, \ldots, \boldsymbol{v}_n^{(a)}\} \tag{3}$$

where FFN_q, FFN_k, FFN_v are single-layer feed-forward neural networks. Then, the attention weight vector $\boldsymbol{a}_k = \{a_1^{(k)}, a_2^{(k)}, \ldots, a_n^{(k)}\} \in \mathbb{R}^n$, where $a_i^{(k)}$ is the weighted score of the i-th word, is computed as the product of $\boldsymbol{Q}$ and $\boldsymbol{K}$, as shown below.

$$\boldsymbol{a}_k = \boldsymbol{K}^\mathsf{T} \boldsymbol{Q} \tag{4}$$

Then, the word with the highest weighted score is chosen as the keyword of the full-sentence answer:

$$i^{(k)} = \underset{i}{\text{argmax}}(a_i^{(k)}) \tag{5}$$

$$\boldsymbol{f}_k = \boldsymbol{v}_{i^{(k)}}^{(a)} \tag{6}$$

However, the argmax operation is non-differentiable. Therefore, we use an approximation of this operation by softmax with temperature.

$$\boldsymbol{f}_k = \boldsymbol{V} \, \text{softmax}(\frac{\boldsymbol{a}_k}{\tau}) \tag{7}$$

where τ is a temperature parameter, and as τ approaches 0, the output of the softmax function becomes a one-hot distribution.

$\mathbf{S}_q$ has the same structure as $\mathbf{S}_a$ up to the point of computing the attention weight vector $\boldsymbol{a}_q$. For the keyword vector, we have the intention to focus on the specific word in the full-sentence answer. Therefore, we use the softmax with temperature. However, for the question vector, there is no need to focus on one word. Therefore, the question vector is calculated as the weighted sum of the attention score:

$$\boldsymbol{f}_q = \boldsymbol{V} \, \text{softmax}(\boldsymbol{a}_q) \tag{8}$$

Then, we applied single-layer feed-forward neural network, followed by layer normalization (Ba et al., 2016) to the output of this module $\boldsymbol{f}_k, \boldsymbol{f}_q$.

3.4 Decoder

Entire Decoder In the entire decoder $\mathbf{D}_{all}$, the full-sentence is reconstructed from the output of the attention scoring modules $\boldsymbol{f}_k$ and $\boldsymbol{f}_q$, i.e., $\boldsymbol{A}_{recon} = \mathbf{D}_{all}(\boldsymbol{f}_k, \boldsymbol{f}_q)$, where $\boldsymbol{A}_{recon}$ denotes the reconstructed full-sentence answer. We use an LSTM as the sentence generator. As the input to the LSTM at each step (x_t), f_k and f_q are concatenated to the output of the previous step as follows:

$$x_0 = W_{x_0}[f_k; f_q] \tag{9}$$

$$x_t = W_x[f_k; f_q; \hat{s}_{t-1}] \tag{10}$$

where $\hat{s}_{t-1}$ is the output of the LSTM at the $t-1$ step, and W_{x_0} and W_x are the learned parameters.

The objective of $\mathbf{D}_{all}$ is defined by the cross-entropy loss:

$$L_{all} = -\sum_{t=1}^{n} \log(p(\hat{s}_t = s_t^{(ans)} \mid s_{1:t-1}^{(ans)})) \tag{11}$$

where $s^{(ans)}$ is the ground-truth full-sentence answer.

Further, word dropout (Bowman et al., 2016), a method of masking input words with a specific probability, is applied. This forces the decoder to generate sentences based on the f_k and f_q rather than relying on the previous word.

Discriminative Decoders $\mathbf{D}_{all}$ attempts to reconstruct the full-sentence answer from f_k and f_q. Thus, $\mathbf{D}_{all}$ allows the feature vectors to contain the answer information. However, the keyword and question information are intended to be represented by f_k and f_q, respectively. Therefore, we designed the discriminative decoders, $\mathbf{D}_a$ and $\mathbf{D}_q$, to generate f_k and f_q, respectively, thus capturing the desired information separately.

$\mathbf{D}_a$ and $\mathbf{D}_q$ reconstruct the full-sentence answer and the question, respectively. This reconstruction is performed with the target of the BoW features of the sentence, rather than the sentence itself. This is because we intend to focus on the content of the sentence and not its sequential information. Sentence reconstruction was also considered as an alternative, but this is difficult to train using LSTM. The BoW feature $b \in \mathbb{R}^{n_s}$ is represented as a vector whose i-th elements is N_i/L_s, where n_s is the vocabulary size, N_i is the number of occurrences of the i-th word, and L_s is the number of the words in the sentence.

The input to these discriminative decoders consists not only of feature vectors, but also auxiliary vectors, the additional features that assist in reconstruction. Specifically, the auxiliary vector for $\mathbf{D}_a$ is the average of the word embedding vectors in the question, f_Q, and, for $\mathbf{D}_q$, the auxiliary vector is the image feature f_I.

We build the decoder as the following fully-connected layers:

$$y_a = W_A[f_k; f_Q] + B_A \tag{12}$$

$$y_q = W_Q[f_q; f_I] + B_Q \tag{13}$$

The loss function for the discriminative decoder is the cross-entropy loss between the ground-truth BoW features and the predicted BoW features:

$$L_a = -\sum_{i=1}^{n_a} b_a[i] \log(\mathrm{softmax}(y_a[i])) \tag{14}$$

$$L_q = -\sum_{i=1}^{n_q} b_q[i] \log(\mathrm{softmax}(y_q[i])) \tag{15}$$

where b denotes the ground-truth of the BoW features, and n_a and n_q are the vocabulary sizes of the answer and the question, respectively.

3.5 Full Objectives

Finally, the overall objective function for the proposed model is written as

$$L = \lambda_{all}L_{all} + \lambda_a L_a + \lambda_q L_q, \tag{16}$$

where λ_{all}, λ_a, and λ_q are hyper-parameters that balance each loss function.

3.6 Implementation Details

In the encoder $\mathbf{E}$, image features of size $2048 \times 14 \times 14$ were extracted from the pool-5 layer of the ResNet152 (He et al., 2016). These were pre-trained on ImageNet, and global pooling was applied to obtain 2048-dimensional features. To encode the question words, we used 300-dimensional GloVe embeddings (Pennington et al., 2014). These were pre-trained on the Wikipedia / Gigaword corpus[1].

To convert each word in the full-sentence answer into f_A, the embedding matrix in the attention scoring module was initialized with the pre-trained GloVe embeddings. The temperature parameter τ is gradually annealed using the schedule $\tau_i = \max(\tau_0\, e^{-ri}, \tau_{min})$, where i is the overall training iteration, and other parameters are set as $\tau_0 = 0.5$, $r = 3.0 \times 10^{-5}$, $\tau_{min} = 0.1$. The LSTM in the $\mathbf{D}_{all}$ has a hidden state of 1024 dimensions. The word dropout rate was set to 0.25.

We used the Adam (Kingma and Ba, 2015) optimizer to train the model, which has an initial learning rate of 1.0×10^{-3}.

---

[1] http://nlp.stanford.edu/projects/glove/

Dataset		Size	Answer length
GQA	train	943,000	6.69
	val	132,062	6.70
FSVQA	train	139,038	6.11
	val	68,265	6.07
VQA v2	train	443,757	1.16
	val	214,354	1.16

Table 1: Basic statistics of the dataset we used. Note that these FSVQA dataset values were taken after pre-processing. Although VQA v2 was not used in this work, it is included in this table for reference.

4 Experimental Setup

4.1 Dataset

We conducted experiments on two datasets: GQA and FSVQA. In Table 1, we present the basic statistics of both datasets.

GQA GQA (Hudson and Manning, 2019) contains 22M questions and answers. The questions and answers are automatically generated from image scene graphs, and the answers include both the single-word answers and the full-sentence answers. The questions and answers in GQA have unbalanced answer distributions. Therefore, we used a balanced version of this dataset, which is down-sampled from the original dataset and contains 1.7M questions. As pre-processing, we removed the periods, commas, and question marks.

FSVQA FSVQA (Shin et al., 2016) contains 370K questions and full-sentence answers. This dataset was built by applying rule-based processing to the VQA v1 dataset (Antol et al., 2015), and captions in the MSCOCO dataset (Lin et al., 2014), to obtain the full-sentence answers. There are ten annotations (i.e., single-word answers) per question in the VQA v1 dataset. Of these, the annotations with the highest frequency is chosen to create full-sentence answers. If all the frequencies are equal, an annotation is chosen at random. Since the authors do not provide the mapping between single-word answers and full-sentence answers, we considered the annotations with the highest frequency as the single-word answers matching the full-sentence answers. Questions for which the highest frequency annotation cannot be determined were filtered out. Following this process, we obtained 139,038 questions for the training set, and 68,265 questions for the validation set.

4.2 Settings

The model performance was determined based on the keyword accuracy and the Mean Rank. Mean Rank is the average rank of the correct keyword when sorting each word in order of the importance score. Mean Rank is formulated as:

$$\text{Mean Rank} = \frac{1}{N} \sum_i rank_i. \tag{17}$$

Here, $rank_i$ is the number representing the keyword rank when the words in the i-th answer sentence are arranged in order of the importance (TF-IDF score or attention score, i.e., $a_i^{(k)}$ in Eqn. 5), and N is the size of the overall samples.

We ran experiments with the various existing unsupervised keyword extraction methods for the comparison: (1) TF-IDF (Ramos, 2003), (2) YAKE (Campos et al., 2020), and (3) EmbedRank (Bennani-Smires et al., 2018). Since YAKE removes the words with less than three characters as preprocessing, the Mean Rank cannot be calculated under the same conditions as other methods. Therefore, the Mean Rank of YAKE is not shown. We also conducted an ablation study to show the importance of $\mathbf{D}_a$ and $\mathbf{D}_q$. In addition, we changed the reconstruction method from BoW estimation to the original sentence generation using LSTM.

5 Experimental Results

The experimental results are shown in Table 2. Also, we provide the accuracy per question types in Appendix A for further analysis. The proposed model, which used BoW estimation in $\mathbf{D}_a$ and $\mathbf{D}_q$, achieves superior performance on almost all metrics and datasets except for the Mean Rank of FSVQA. As can be seen in the results of the ablation study, this superior performance is achieved even without $\mathbf{D}_a$ and $\mathbf{D}_q$, which demonstrates the effectiveness of the proposed reconstruction-based method. When using LSTM in $\mathbf{D}_a$ and $\mathbf{D}_q$, the accuracy and mean rank worsens as compared to those of the proposed model, which reconstructs the BoW in those modules. This is considered to be because sentence reconstruction with LSTM requires management of the sequential information of the sentence, which is more complex than BoW estimation. Since we intended to focus on the contents of the sentence, the BoW is more suitable for these modules.

| | **GQA** | | **FSVQA** | |
Model	**Accuracy** ($\uparrow$)	**Mean Rank** ($\downarrow$)	**Accuracy** ($\uparrow$)	**Mean Rank** ($\downarrow$)
TF-IDF	0.275	2.86	0.278	3.22
YAKE	0.269	–	0.107	–
EmbedRank	0.306	2.15	0.302	**2.32**
Ours	**0.429** $\pm$ **0.03**	**2.04** $\pm$ **0.10**	**0.351** $\pm$ **0.04**	2.38 $\pm$ 0.14
Ours w/o $\mathbf{D}_q$	0.318 $\pm$ 0.02	2.44 $\pm$ 0.04	0.298 $\pm$ 0.03	2.67 $\pm$ 0.05
Ours w/o $\mathbf{D}_a$, $\mathbf{D}_q$	0.350 $\pm$ 0.06	3.01 $\pm$ 0.49	0.347 $\pm$ 0.05	2.49 $\pm$ 0.21
Ours (LSTM $\mathbf{D}_a$, $\mathbf{D}_q$)	0.329 $\pm$ 0.01	2.36 $\pm$ 0.04	0.347 $\pm$ 0.01	3.35 $\pm$ 0.11

Table 2: Keyword extraction performanc on GQA and FSVQA. Higher accuracies and lower Mean Ranks are desirable. We conducted experiments three times using the proposed method. Note that comparison methods are deterministic algorithms, experiments with them were conducted only once.

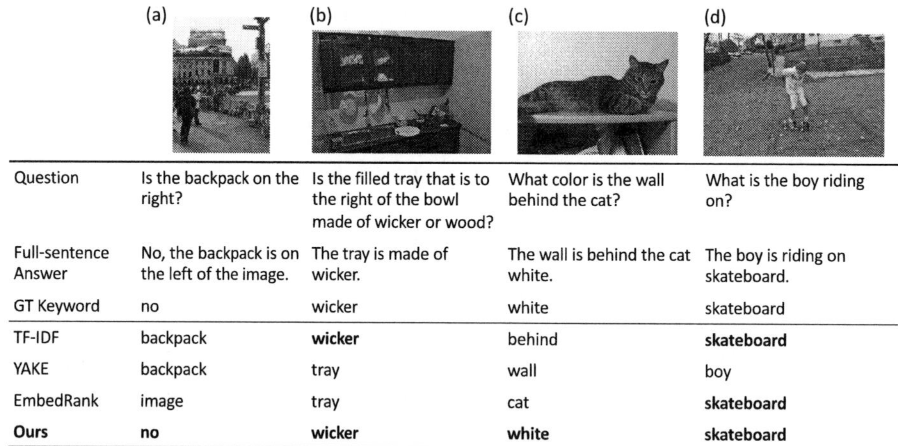

	(a)	(b)	(c)	(d)
Question	Is the backpack on the right?	Is the filled tray that is to the right of the bowl made of wicker or wood?	What color is the wall behind the cat?	What is the boy riding on?
Full-sentence Answer	No, the backpack is on the left of the image.	The tray is made of wicker.	The wall is behind the cat white.	The boy is riding on skateboard.
GT Keyword	no	wicker	white	skateboard
TF-IDF	backpack	**wicker**	behind	**skateboard**
YAKE	backpack	tray	wall	boy
EmbedRank	image	tray	cat	**skateboard**
Ours	**no**	**wicker**	**white**	**skateboard**

Figure 4: Examples of the keyword extraction results in the GQA dataset (a, b) and the FSVQA dataset (c, d).

We provide some examples in Figure 4. The examples on the left and right are from GQA and FSVQA, respectively. Since the statistical methods such as TF-IDF tend to choose rarer words as keywords, they are likely to fail if the keyword is a common word (Figure 4 (a), (c)). On the other hand, the model proposed herein can accurately extract keywords even in such cases.

6 Conclusion

In this paper, we proposed the novel task of unsupervised keyword extraction from full-sentence VQA. A novel model was designed to handle this task based on information decomposition of full-sentence answers and the reconstruction of questions and answers. Both qualitative and quantitative experiments show that our model successfully extracts the keyword of the full-sentence answer with no keyword supervision.

In future work, the extracted keywords will be utilized in other tasks, such as VQA, object classification, or object detection. This work could also be combined with recent works on VQG (Uehara et al., 2018; Shen et al., 2019). In these works, the system generates questions to acquire information from humans. However, they assume that the answers are obtained as single words, which will pose a problem when applying it to the real-world question answering. By combining these studies with our research, an intelligent system can ask humans about unseen objects and learn new knowledge from the answer, even if the answer consists of more than a single word.

Acknowledgement This work was partially supported by JST CREST Grant Number JP-MJCR1403, and partially supported by JSPS KAKENHI Grant Number JP19H01115 and JP20H05556. We would like to thank Yang Li, Sho Maeoki, Sho Inayoshi, and Antonio Tejero-de-Pablos for helpful discussions.

References

Stanislaw Antol, Aishwarya Agrawal, Jiasen Lu, Margaret Mitchell, Dhruv Batra, C. Lawrence Zitnick, and Devi Parikh. 2015. Vqa: Visual question answering. In *ICCV*.

Jimmy Lei Ba, Jamie Ryan Kiros, and Geoffrey E Hinton. 2016. Layer normalization. *arXiv preprint arXiv:1607.06450*.

Dzmitry Bahdanau, Kyunghyun Cho, and Yoshua Bengio. 2015. Neural Machine Translation by Jointly Learning to Align and Translate. In *ICLR*.

Kamil Bennani-Smires, Claudiu Musat, Andreea Hossmann, Michael Baeriswyl, and Martin Jaggi. 2018. Simple unsupervised keyphrase extraction using sentence embeddings. In *CoNLL*.

Samuel R. Bowman, Luke Vilnis, Oriol Vinyals, Andrew Dai, Rafal Jozefowicz, and Samy Bengio. 2016. Generating sentences from a continuous space. In *CoNLL*.

Ricardo Campos, Vtor Mangaravite, Arian Pasquali, Alpio Jorge, Clia Nunes, and Adam Jatowt. 2020. Yake! keyword extraction from single documents using multiple local features. *Information Sciences*.

Abhishek Das, Satwik Kottur, Khushi Gupta, Avi Singh, Deshraj Yadav, Jose M. F. Moura, Devi Parikh, and Dhruv Batra. 2017. Visual dialog. In *CVPR*.

Jacob Devlin, Ming-Wei Chang, Kenton Lee, and Kristina Toutanova. 2019. BERT: Pre-training of deep bidirectional transformers for language understanding. In *NAACL-HLT*.

Yash Goyal, Tejas Khot, Douglas Summers-Stay, Dhruv Batra, and Devi Parikh. 2017. Making the V in VQA matter: Elevating the role of image understanding in Visual Question Answering. In *CVPR*.

Kaiming He, Xiangyu Zhang, Shaoqing Ren, and Jian Sun. 2016. Deep residual learning for image recognition. In *CVPR*.

Drew A. Hudson and Christopher D. Manning. 2019. Gqa: A new dataset for real-world visual reasoning and compositional question answering. In *CVPR*.

Diederik P Kingma and Jimmy Ba. 2015. Adam: A method for stochastic optimization. In *ICLR*.

Ranjay Krishna, Yuke Zhu, Oliver Groth, Justin Johnson, Kenji Hata, Joshua Kravitz, Stephanie Chen, Yannis Kalantidis, Li-Jia Li, David A Shamma, et al. 2017. Visual genome: Connecting language and vision using crowdsourced dense image annotations. *IJCV*.

Tsung-Yi Lin, Michael Maire, Serge Belongie, James Hays, Pietro Perona, Deva Ramanan, Piotr Dollár, and C Lawrence Zitnick. 2014. Microsoft coco: Common objects in context. In *ECCV*.

Rada Mihalcea and Paul Tarau. 2004. TextRank: Bringing order into text. In *EMNLP*.

Ishan Misra, Ross Girshick, Rob Fergus, Martial Hebert, Abhinav Gupta, and Laurens van der Maaten. 2018. Learning by asking questions. In *CVPR*.

Jeffrey Pennington, Richard Socher, and Christopher Manning. 2014. Glove: Global vectors for word representation. In *EMNLP*.

Juan Ramos. 2003. Using TF-IDF to Determine Word Relevance in Document Queries. In *the first instructional conference on machine learning*.

Tingke Shen, Amlan Kar, and Sanja Fidler. 2019. Learning to caption images through a lifetime by asking questions. In *ICCV*.

Andrew Shin, Yoshitaka Ushiku, and Tatsuya Harada. 2016. The color of the cat is gray: 1 million full-sentences visual question answering (fsvqa). *arXiv preprint arXiv:1609.06657*.

Kohei Uehara, Antonio Tejero-De-Pablos, Yoshitaka Ushiku, and Tatsuya Harada. 2018. Visual question generation for class acquisition of unknown objects. In *ECCV*.

Ashish Vaswani, Noam Shazeer, Niki Parmar, Jakob Uszkoreit, Llion Jones, Aidan N Gomez, Łukasz Kaiser, and Illia Polosukhin. 2017. Attention is all you need. In *NeurIPS*.

Xiaojun Wan and Jianguo Xiao. Single document keyphrase extraction using neighborhood knowledge.

Xing Wu, Zhikang Du, and Yike Guo. 2018. A visual attention-based keyword extraction for document classification. *Multimedia Tools and Applications*, 77(19):25355–25367.

MAST: Multimodal Abstractive Summarization with Trimodal Hierarchical Attention

Aman Khullar[*]
IIIT Hyderabad
Hyderabad, India
aman.khullar@iiit.ac.in

Udit Arora[*]
New York University
New York, NY, USA
uditarora@nyu.edu

Abstract

This paper presents MAST, a new model for Multimodal Abstractive Text Summarization that utilizes information from all three modalities – text, audio and video – in a multimodal video. Prior work on multimodal abstractive text summarization only utilized information from the text and video modalities. We examine the usefulness and challenges of deriving information from the audio modality and present a sequence-to-sequence trimodal hierarchical attention-based model that overcomes these challenges by letting the model pay more attention to the text modality. MAST outperforms the current state of the art model (video-text) by 2.51 points in terms of Content F1 score and 1.00 points in terms of Rouge-L score on the How2 dataset for multimodal language understanding.

1 Introduction

In recent years, there has been a dramatic rise in information access through videos, facilitated by a proportional increase in the number of video-sharing platforms. This has led to an enormous amount of information accessible to help with our day-to-day activities. The accompanying transcripts or the automatic speech-to-text transcripts for these videos present the same information in the textual modality. However, all this information is often lengthy and sometimes incomprehensible because of verbosity. These limitations in user experience and information access are improved upon by the recent advancements in the field of multimodal text summarization.

Multimodal text summarization is the task of condensing this information from the interacting modalities into an output summary. This generated output summary may be unimodal or multimodal (Zhu et al., 2018). The textual summary

may, in turn, be extractive or abstractive. The task of extractive multimodal text summarization involves selection and concatenation of the most important sentences in the input text without altering the sentences or their sequence in any way. Li et al. (2017) made the selection of these important sentences using visual and acoustic cues from the corresponding visual and auditory modalities. On the other hand, the task of abstractive multimodal text summarization involves identification of the theme of the input data and the generation of words based on the deeper understanding of the material. This is a tougher problem to solve which has been alleviated with the advancements in the abstractive text summarization techniques – Rush et al. (2015), See et al. (2017) and Liu and Lapata (2019). Sanabria et al. (2018) introduced the How2 dataset for large-scale multimodal language understanding, and Palaskar et al. (2019) were able to produce state of the art results for multimodal abstractive text summarization on the dataset. They utilized a sequence-to-sequence hierarchical attention based technique (Libovický and Helcl, 2017) for combining textual and image features to produce the textual summary from the multimodal input. Moreover, they used speech for generating the speech-to-text transcriptions using pre-trained speech recognizers, however it did not supplement the other modalities.

Though the previous work in abstractive multimodal text summarization has been promising, it has not yet been able to capture the effects of combining the audio features. Our work improves upon this shortcoming by examining the benefits and challenges of introducing the audio modality as part of our solution. We hypothesize that the audio modality can impart additional useful information for the text summarization task by letting the model pay more attention to words that are spoken with a certain tone or level of emphasis. Through our

---

[*] indicates equal contribution
Aman Khullar is presently at Gram Vaani

Proceedings of the First International Workshop on Natural Language Processing Beyond Text, pages 60–69
Online, November 20, 2020. ©2020 Association for Computational Linguistics
http://www.aclweb.org/anthology/W23-20%2d

Original text: let's talk now about how to bait a tip up hook with a maggot. typically, you're going to be using this for pan fish. not a real well known or common technique but on a given day it could be the difference between not catching fish and catching fish. all you do, you take your maggot, you can use meal worms, as well, which are much bigger, which are probably more well suited for this because this is a rather large hook. you would just, again, put that hook right through the maggot. with a big hook like this, i would probably put ten of these on it, just line the whole thing. this is going to be more of a technique for pan fish, such as, perch and sunfish, some of your smaller fish but if you had maggots, like this , or a meal worm, or two, on a hook like this, this would be a fantastic setup for trout, as well.
Text only: ice fishing is used for ice fishing. learn about ice fishing bait with tips from an experienced fisherman artist in this free fishing video.
Video-Text: learn about the ice fishing bait in this ice fishing lesson from an experienced fisherman.
MAST: maggots are good for catching perch. learn more about ice fishing bait in this ice fishing lesson from an experienced fisherman.

Table 1: Comparison of outputs by using different modality configurations for a test video example. Frequently occurring words are highlighted in red, which are easier for a simpler model to predict but do not contribute much in terms of useful content. The summary generated by the MAST model contains more content words as compared to the baselines.

experiments, we were able to prove that not all modalities contribute equally to the output. We found a higher contribution of text, followed by video and then by audio. This formed the motivation for our MAST model, which places higher importance on text input while generating the output summary. MAST is able to produce a more illustrative summary of the original text (see Table 1) and achieves state of the art results.

In summary, our primary contributions are:

- Introduction of audio modality for abstractive multimodal text summarization.

- Examining the challenges of utilizing audio information and understanding its contribution in the generated summary.

- Proposition of a novel state of the art model, MAST, for the task of multimodal abstractive text summarization.

2 Methodology

In this section we describe (1) the dataset used, (2) the modalities, and (3) our MAST model's architecture. The code for our model is available online[1].

[1] https://github.com/amankhullar/mast

2.1 Dataset

We use the 300h version of the How2 dataset (Sanabria et al., 2018) of open-domain videos. The dataset consists of about 300 hours of short instructional videos spanning different domains such as cooking, sports, indoor/outdoor activities, music, and more. A human-generated transcript accompanies each video, and a 2 to 3 sentence summary is available for every video, written to generate interest in a potential viewer. The 300h version is used instead of the 2000h version because the audio modality information is only available for the 300h subset.

The dataset is divided into the training, validation and test sets. The training set consists of 13,168 videos totaling 298.2 hours. The validation set consists of 150 videos totaling 3.2 hours, and the test set consists of 175 videos totaling 3.7 hours. A more detailed description of the dataset has been given by Sanabria et al. (2018). For our experiments, we took 12,798 videos for the training set, 520 videos for the validation set and 127 videos for the test set.

2.2 Modalities

We use the following three inputs corresponding to the three different modalities used:

- **Audio**: We use the concatenation of 40-dimensional Kaldi (Povey et al., 2011) filter bank features from 16kHz raw audio using a time window of 25ms with 10ms frame shift and the 3-dimensional pitch features extracted from the dataset to obtain the final sequence of 43-dimensional audio features.

- **Text**: We use the transcripts corresponding to each video. All texts are normalized and lower-cased.

- **Video**: We use a 2048-dimensional feature vector per group of 16 frames, which is extracted from the videos using a ResNeXt-101 3D CNN trained to recognize 400 different actions (Hara et al., 2018). This results in a sequence of feature vectors per video.

2.3 Multimodal Abstractive Summarization with Trimodal Hierarchical Attention

Figure 1 shows the architecture of our Multimodal Abstractive Summarization with Trimodal Hierarchical Attention (MAST) model. The model consists of three components - Modality Encoders, Tri-

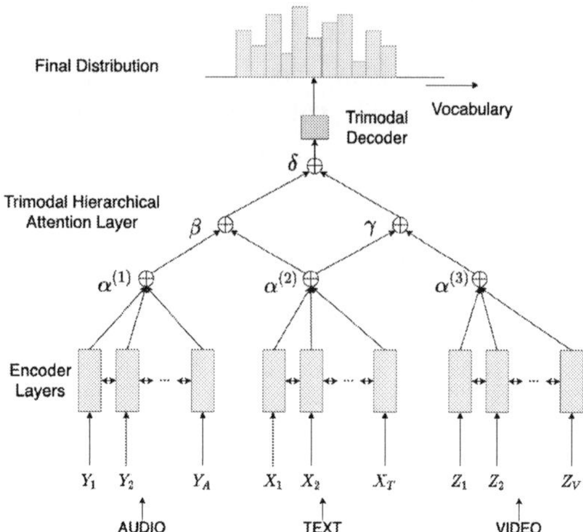

Figure 1: Multimodal Abstractive Summarization with Trimodal Hierarchical Attention (MAST) architecture: MAST is a sequence to sequence model that uses information from all three modalities – audio, text and video. The modality information is encoded using Modality Encoders, followed by a Trimodal Hierarchical Attention Layer, which combines this information using a three-level hierarchical attention approach. It attends to two pairs of modalities (δ) (Audio-Text and Video-Text) followed by the modality in each pair (β and γ), followed by the individual features within each modality (α). The decoder utilizes this combination of modalities to generate the output over the vocabulary.

modal Hierarchical Attention Layer and the Trimodal Decoder.

2.3.1 Modality Encoders

The text is embedded with an embedding layer and encoded using a bidirectional GRU encoder. The audio and video features are encoded using bidirectional LSTM encoders. This gives us the individual output encoding corresponding to all modalities at each encoder timestep. The tokens $t_i^{(k)}$ corresponding to modality k are encoded using the corresponding modality encoders and produce a sequence of hidden states $h_i^{(k)}$ for each encoder time step (i).

2.3.2 Trimodal Hierarchical Attention Layer

We build upon the hierarchical attention approach proposed by Libovický and Helcl (2017) to combine the modalities. On each decoder timestep i, the attention distribution (α) and the context vector for the k-th modality is first computed indepen-

dently as in Bahdanau et al. (2014):

$$e_{ij}^{(k)} = v_a^{(k)\mathrm{T}}\tanh(W_a^{(k)}s_i + U_a^{(k)}h_j^{(k)} + b_{att}^{(k)}) \quad (1)$$

$$\alpha_{ij}^{(k)} = \mathrm{softmax}(e_{ij}^{(k)}) \quad (2)$$

$$c_i^{(k)} = \sum_{\substack{j=1, \\ k\in\{\text{audio, text, video}\}}}^{N_k} \alpha_{ij}^{(k)} h_j^{(k)} \quad (3)$$

Where s_i is the decoder hidden state at i-th decoder timestep, $h_j^{(k)}$ is the encoder hidden state at j-th encoder timestep, N_k is the number of encoder timesteps for the k-th modality and $e_{ij}^{(k)}$ is attention energy corresponding to them. W_a and U_a are trainable projection matrices, v_a is a weight vector and b_{att} is the bias term.

We now look at two different strategies of combining information from the modalities. The first is a simple extension of the hierarchical attention combination. The second is the strategy used in MAST, which combines modalities using three levels of hierarchical attention.

1. TrimodalH2: To obtain our first baseline model (*TrimodalH2*), with 2 level attention hierarchy, the context vectors for all three modalities are combined using a second layer of attention mechanism and its context vector is computed separately by using hierarchical attention combination as in Libovický and Helcl (2017):

$$e_i^{(k)} = v_b^T\tanh(W_b s_i + U_b^{(k)}c_i^{(k)}) \quad (4)$$

$$\eta_i^{(k)} = \mathrm{softmax}(e_i^{(k)}) \quad (5)$$

$$c_i = \sum_{k\in\{\text{audio, text, video}\}} \eta_i^{(k)} U_c^{(k)} c_i^{(k)} \quad (6)$$

where $\eta^{(k)}$ is the hierarchical attention distribution over the modalities, $c_i^{(k)}$ is the context vector of the k-th modality encoder, v_b and W_b are shared parameters across modalities, and $U_b^{(k)}$ and $U_c^{(k)}$ are modality-specific projection matrices.

2. MAST: To obtain our MAST model, the context vectors for audio-text and text-video are combined using a second layer of hierarchical attention mechanisms (β and γ) and their context vectors are computed separately. These context-vectors are then combined using the third hierarchical attention mechanism (δ).

1. Audio-Text:

$$e_i^{(k)} = v_d^T \tanh(W_d s_i + U_d^{(k)} c_i^{(k)}) \qquad (7)$$

$$\beta_i^{(k)} = \text{softmax}(e_i^{(k)}) \qquad (8)$$

$$d_i^{(1)} = \sum_{k \in \{\text{audio, text}\}} \beta_i^{(k)} U_e^{(k)} c_i^{(k)} \qquad (9)$$

2. Video-Text:

$$e_i^{(k)} = v_f^T \tanh(W_f s_i + U_f^{(k)} c_i^{(k)}) \qquad (10)$$

$$\gamma_i^{(k)} = \text{softmax}(e_i^{(k)}) \qquad (11)$$

$$d_i^{(2)} = \sum_{k \in \{\text{video, text}\}} \gamma_i^{(k)} U_g^{(k)} c_i^{(k)} \qquad (12)$$

where $d_i^{(l)}$, $l \in \{\text{audio-text, video-text}\}$ is the context vector obtained for the corresponding pair-wise modality combination.

Finally, these audio-text and video-text context vectors are combined using the third and final attention layer (δ). With this trimodal hierarchical attention architecture, we combine the textual modality twice with the other two modalities in a pair-wise manner, and this allows the model to pay more attention to the textual modality while incorporating the benefits of the other two modalities.

$$e_i^{(l)} = v_h^T \tanh(W_g s_i + U_h^{(l)} d_i^{(l)}) \qquad (13)$$

$$\delta_i^{(l)} = \text{softmax}(e_i^{(l)}) \qquad (14)$$

$$c_i^f = \sum_{l \in \{\text{audio-text, video-text}\}} \delta_i^{(l)} U_m^{(l)} d_i^{(l)} \qquad (15)$$

where c_i^f is the final context vector at i-th decoder timestep.

2.3.3 Trimodal Decoder

We use a GRU-based conditional decoder (Firat and Cho, 2016) to generate the final vocabulary distribution at each timestep. At each timestep, the decoder has the aggregate information from all the modalities. The trimodal decoder focuses on the modality combination, followed by the individual modality, then focuses on the particular information inside that modality. Finally, it uses this information along with information from previous timesteps, which is passed on to two linear layers to generate the next word from the vocabulary.

3 Experiments

We train Trimodal Hierarchical Attention (MAST) and TrimodalH2 models on the 300h version of the How2 dataset, using all three modalities. We also train Hierarchical Attention models considering Audio-Text and Video-Text modalities, as well as simple Seq2Seq models with attention for each modality individually as baselines. As observed by Palaskar et al. (2019), the Pointer Generator model (See et al., 2017) does not perform as well as Seq2Seq models on this dataset, hence we do not use that as a baseline in our experiments. We consider another transformer-based baseline for the text modality, BertSumAbs (Liu and Lapata, 2019).

For all our experiments (except for the BerSumAbs baseline), we use the *nmtpytorch* toolkit (Caglayan et al., 2017). The source and the target vocabulary consists of 49,329 words on which we train our word embeddings. We use the NLL loss and the Adam optimizer (Kingma and Ba, 2014) with learning rate 0.0004 and trained the models for 50 epochs. We generate our summaries using beam search with a beam size of 5, and then evaluate them using the ROUGE metric (Lin, 2004) and the Content F1 metric (Palaskar et al., 2019).

In our experiments, the text is embedded with an embedding layer of size 256 and then encoded using a bidirectional GRU encoder (Cho et al., 2014) with a hidden layer of size 128, which gives us a 256-dimensional output encoding corresponding to the text at each timestep. The audio and video frames are encoded using bidirectional LSTM encoders (Hochreiter and Schmidhuber, 1997) with a hidden layer of size 128, which gives a 256-dimensional output encoding corresponding to the audio and video features at each timestep. Finally, the GRU-based conditional decoder uses a hidden layer of size 128 followed by two linear layers which transform the decoder output to generate the final output vocabulary distribution.

To improve generalization of our model, we use two dropout layers within the Text Encoder and one dropout layer on the output of the conditional decoder, all with a probability of 0.35. We also use implicit regularization by using early stopping mechanism on the validation loss with a patience of 40 epochs.

3.1 Challenges of using audio modality

The first challenge comes with obtaining a good representation of the audio modality that adds value beyond the text modality for the task of text summarization. As found by Mohamed (2014), DNN acoustic models prefer features that smoothly change both in time and frequency, like the log mel-frequency spectral coefficients (MFSC), to the decorrelated mel-frequency cepstral coefficients (MFCC). MFSC features make it easier for DNNs to discover linear relations as well as higher order causes of the input data, leading to better overall system performance. Hence we do not consider MFCC features in our experiments and use the filter bank features instead.

The second challenge arises due to the larger number of parameters that a model needs when handling the audio information. The number of parameters in the Video-Text baseline is 16.95 million as compared to 32.08 million when we add audio. This is because of the high number of input timesteps in the audio modality encoder, which makes learning trickier and more time-consuming.

To demonstrate these challenges, as an experiment, we group the audio features across input timesteps into bins with an average of 30 consecutive timesteps and train our MAST model. This makes the number of audio timesteps comparable to the number of video and text timesteps. While we observe an improvement in computational efficiency, it achieves a lower performance than the baseline Video-Text model as described in Table 2 (MAST-Binned). We also train Audio only and Audio-Text models which fail to beat the Text only baseline. We observe that the generated summaries of the Audio only model are similar and repetitive, indicating that the model failed to learn useful information relevant to the task of text summarization.

4 Results and Discussion

| Model | ROUGE | | | Content |
Name	1	2	L	F1
Text Only	46.01	25.16	39.98	33.45
BertSumAbs	29.68	11.74	22.58	31.53
Video Only	39.23	19.82	34.17	27.06
Audio Only	29.16	12.36	28.86	26.65
Audio-Text	34.56	15.22	31.63	28.36
Video-Text	48.40	27.97	42.23	32.89
TrimodalH2	47.85	28.46	42.17	**35.65**
MAST-Binned	46.22	25.94	40.34	33.56
MAST	**48.85**	**29.51**	**43.23**	35.40

Table 2: Results for different configurations. MAST outperforms all baseline models in terms of ROUGE scores, and obtains a higher Content-F1 score than all baselines while obtaining a score close to the TrimodalH2 model.

4.1 Preliminaries

Our results are given in Table 2. To demonstrate the contribution of various modalities towards the output summary, we experiment with the three modalities taken individually as well as in combination. Text only, Video only and the Audio only are attention-based S2S models (Bahdanau et al., 2014) with their respective modality features taken as encoder inputs. To situate the efficacy of the encoder-decoder architecture for our task, we use the BertSumAbs (Liu and Lapata, 2019) as a BERT based baseline for abstractive text summarization. Audio-Text and the Video-Text are S2S models with hierarchical attention layer. The Video-Text model as presented by Palaskar et al. (2019) has been compared on the 300h version instead of the 2000h version of the dataset because the audio modality is only available in the former. TrimodalH2 model, adds the audio modality in the second-level of hierarchical attention. MAST-Binned model groups the features of the audio modality for computational efficiency. These models show alternative methods for utilizing audio modality information.

We evaluate our models with the ROUGE metric (Lin, 2004) and the Content F1 metric (Palaskar et al., 2019). The Content F1 metric is the F1 score of the content words in the summaries based on a monolingual alignment. It is calculated using the METEOR toolkit (Denkowski and Lavie, 2011) by setting zero weight to function words (δ), equal weights to Precision and Recall (α), and no cross-over penalty (γ) for generated words. Additionally, a set of catchphrases like the words - in, this, free, video, learn, how, tips, expert - which appear in most summaries and act like function words instead of content words are removed from the reference and hypothesis summaries as a post-processing step. It ignores the fluency of the output, but gives an estimate of the amount of useful content words the model is able to capture in the output.

4.2 Discussion

As observed from the scores for the Text Only model, the text modality contains the most amount of information relevant to the final summary, followed by the video and the audio modalities. The scores obtained by combining the audio-text and video-text modalities also indicate the same. The transformer-based model, BertSumAbs, fails to perform well because of the smaller amount of text

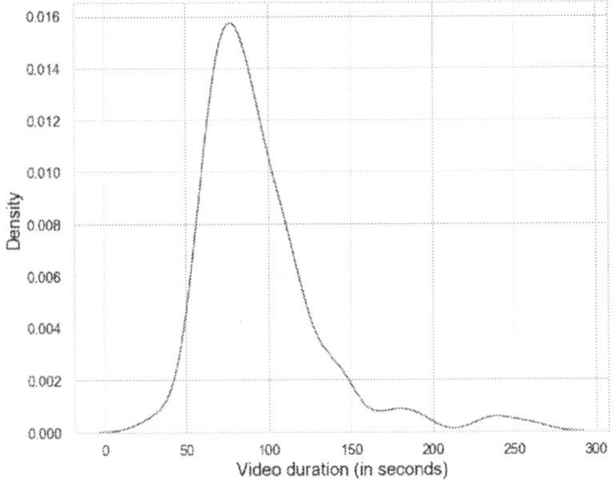

Figure 2: Distribution of the duration of videos (in seconds) in the test set.

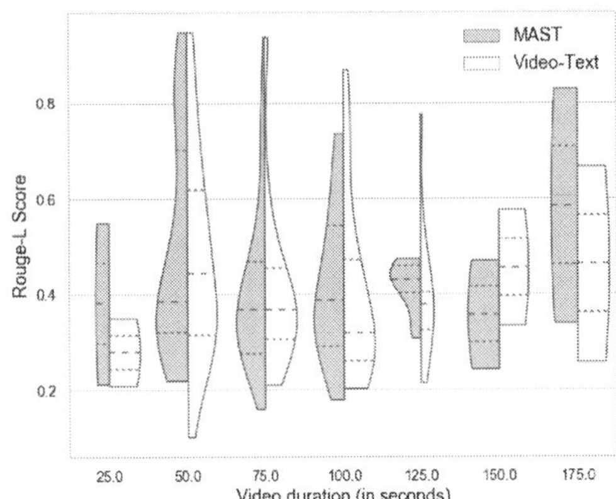

Figure 3: Distribution of Rouge-L scores of summaries produced for different video durations (in seconds) for MAST and Video-Text baseline. The videos are binned into groups of 25 seconds by duration and the distribution of Rouge-L scores within each group is shown using density plots. The dotted lines inside each group show the quartile distribution.

data available to fine-tune the model.

We also observe that combining the text and audio modalities leads to a lower ROUGE score than the Text Only model, which indicates that the plain hierarchical attention model fails to learn well over the audio modality by itself. This observation is in line with the result obtained by the TrimodalH2 model, where we simply extend the hierarchical attention approach to three modalities.

4.2.1 Usefulness of audio modality

The MAST and the TrimodalH2 models achieve a higher Content F1 score than the Video-Text baseline, indicating that the model learns to extract more useful content by utilizing information from the audio modality corresponding to the characteristics of speech, in line with our initial hypothesis as illustrated in Table 1

However, the TrimodalH2 model, which simply adds the audio modality in the second level of hierarchical attention, fails to outperform the Video-Text baseline in terms of ROUGE scores. Our architecture lets the MAST model choose between paying attention to a different combination of modalities with the text modality. This forces the model to pay more attention to the text modality, thereby overcoming the shortcoming of the TrimodalH2 model and achieving better ROUGE scores, while maintaining a similar Content F1 score when compared to TrimodalH2.

4.2.2 Attention distribution across modalities

To understand the importance of individual modalities and their combinations, we plot their attention distribution at different levels of attention hierarchy across the decoder timesteps. Figure 4a corresponds to attention weights as calculated in

equation 14 while figures 4b and 4c correspond to the product of attention weights between equations 11, 8 and corresponding weight in equation 14 for each decoder timestep. The final attention within each individual modality at each decoder timestep is calculated by multiplying the corresponding cumulative attention weights obtained at level 2 of attention hierarchy with the attention weights obtained in equation 2 (figures 4d to 4f). The attention weights assigned to the audio modality have been added across input timesteps (group size of 30) in order to obtain a more interpretable visualization.

Through these visualizations, we observe that the text modality dominates the generation of the output summary while giving lesser attention to the audio and video modalities (the latter being more important). These findings support the extra importance being given to the text modality in the MAST model during its interaction with the other modalities. Figures 4b and 4d highlight the modest gains through the audio modality and the challenge in its appropriate usage.

4.2.3 Performance across video durations

We also look at how our model performs for different video durations in our test set. Figure 3 shows the variation in the Rouge-L scores across different videos for MAST and the Video-Text baseline. The figure shows videos binned into seven groups of 25 seconds by duration. We can observe from the quartile distribution that MAST outperforms the baseline in five out of the seven groups, gives similar performance for videos with a duration between 75-100 seconds, and underperforms for videos with a duration between 150-175 seconds. However, overall, by looking at the distribution of the duration of videos in our test set (Figure 2), we can observe that MAST outperforms the baseline for a vast majority of videos across durations.

5 Related Work

5.1 Abstractive text summarization

Abstractive summarization of documents was traditionally achieved by paraphrasing and fusing multiple sentences along with their grammatical rewriting (Woodsend and Lapata, 2012). This was later improved by taking inspiration from human comprehension capabilities when Fang and Teufel (2014) implemented the model of human comprehension and summarization proposed by Kintsch and Van Dijk (1978). They did this by identifying these concepts in text through the application of co-reference resolution, named entity recognition and semantic similarity detection, implemented as a two-step competition.

The real stimulus to the field of abstractive summarization was provided by the application of neural encoder-decoder architectures. Rush et al. (2015) were among the first to achieve state-of-the-art results on Gigaword (Graff et al., 2003) and the DUC-2004 (Over et al., 2007) datasets and established the importance of end-to-end deep learning models for abstractive summarization. Their work was later improved upon by See et al. (2017) where they used copying from the source text to remove the problem of incorrect generation of facts in the summary, as well as a coverage mechanism to curb the problem of repetition of words in the generated summary.

5.2 Pretrained language models

Another breakthrough for the field of natural language processing came with the use of pre-trained language models for carrying out various language downstream tasks. Pre-trained language models like BERT (Devlin et al., 2018) introduced masked language modelling, which allowed models to learn interactions between left and right context words. These models have significantly changed the way word embeddings are generated by training contextual embeddings rather than static embeddings. Liu and Lapata (2019) presented how BERT could be used for text summarization and proposed a new fine-tuning schedule for abstractive summarization which adopted different optimizers for the encoder and the decoder to alleviate the mismatch between the two. BERT models typically require large amounts of annotated data to produce state-of-the-art results. Recent works, like GAN-BERT by Croce et al. (2020) focus on solving this problem.

5.3 Advancements in speech recognition and computer vision

Parallel advancements in the field of speech recognition and computer vision have been able to give us successful methods to extract useful features of speech and images. Peddinti et al. (2015) built a robust acoustic model for speech recognition using a time-delay neural network. They were able to achieve state-of-the-art results in the IARPA ASpIRE Challenge. Similarly, with the advancements of convolutional neural networks, the field of computer vision has progressed significantly. He et al. (2016) demonstrated the strength of deep residual networks which learned residual functions with reference to the layers and were able to achieve state-of-the art results on the ImageNet dataset. Hara et al. (2018) showed that simple 3D Convolutional Neural Network (CNN) architectures outperform complex 2D architectures and trained a ResNeXt-101 3D CNN to recognize 400 different human actions on the Kinetics dataset (Kay et al., 2017).

5.4 Summarization beyond text

The advancements in these fields have in turn also facilitated text summarization. Rott and Červa (2016) used only the input audio to generate textual summaries while Sah et al. (2017) were among the first to show the possibility of summarizing long videos and then annotating the summarized video to obtain a textual summary. These models, however, were not able to capture the information of other modalities to obtain the output textual summary and hence their limitations led to the increasing use of multimodal data. A major hindrance in the field of multimodal text summarization was the lack of datasets. Li et al. (2017) created an asynchronous benchmark dataset with human-annotated summaries for 500 videos. Sanabria et al. (2018) then released a large-scale dataset for instructional videos. JN et al. (2020) and Zhu et al. (2018) presented multimodal text summarization models using textual and visual modalities as input and multimodal outputs of summarized text and video. Palaskar et al. (2019) used How2 dataset

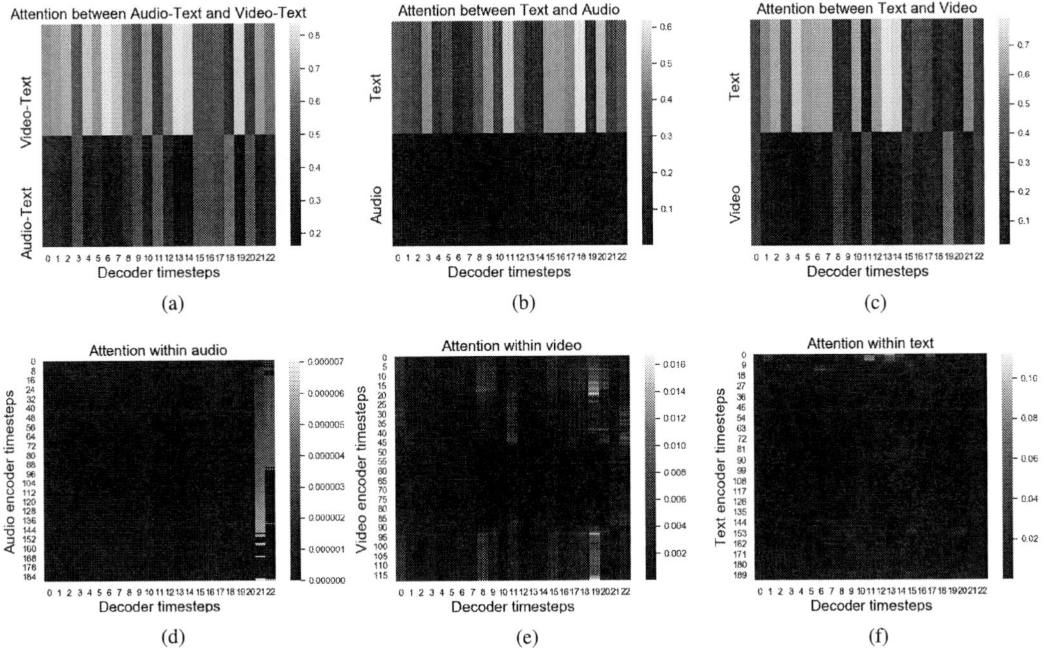

Figure 4: Visualization of attention weights in the Trimodal Hierarchical Attention layer for a sample video in the test set. Figures 4a to 4c show the varying attention distribution on different combinations of modalities across the decoder timesteps. Figures 4d to 4f show the attention distribution on the encoder timesteps for each modality across the decoder timesteps. This shows the usefulness of each modality for the generation of the summary.

to present an abstractive summary of open-domain videos. These models, however, are not completely multimodal since they do not utilise the audio information. A major focus of our work is to highlight the importance of using audio data as input and incorporate it in a truly multimodal manner.

6 Conclusion

In this work[2], we presented MAST, a state of the art sequence to sequence based model that uses information from all three modalities – audio, text and video – to generate abstractive multimodal text summaries. It uses a Trimodal Hierarchical Attention layer to utilize information from all modalities. We explored the role played by adding the audio modality and compared MAST with several baseline models, demonstrating the effectiveness of our approach.

In the future, we would like to extend this work by looking at alternate audio modality representations including using neural networks for audio feature extraction, and also explore the use of transformers for an end to end attention based learning. We also aim to explore the application of MAST to

other multimodal tasks like translation.

References

Dzmitry Bahdanau, Kyunghyun Cho, and Yoshua Bengio. 2014. Neural machine translation by jointly learning to align and translate. *arXiv preprint arXiv:1409.0473*.

Ozan Caglayan, Mercedes García-Martínez, Adrien Bardet, Walid Aransa, Fethi Bougares, and Loïc Barrault. 2017. Nmtpy: A flexible toolkit for advanced neural machine translation systems. *The Prague Bulletin of Mathematical Linguistics*, 109(1):15–28.

Kyunghyun Cho, Bart Van Merriënboer, Caglar Gulcehre, Dzmitry Bahdanau, Fethi Bougares, Holger Schwenk, and Yoshua Bengio. 2014. Learning phrase representations using rnn encoder-decoder for statistical machine translation. *arXiv preprint arXiv:1406.1078*.

Danilo Croce, Giuseppe Castellucci, and Roberto Basili. 2020. Gan-bert: Generative adversarial learning for robust text classification with a bunch of labeled examples. In *Proceedings of the 58th Annual Meeting of the Association for Computational Linguistics*, pages 2114–2119.

Michael Denkowski and Alon Lavie. 2011. Meteor 1.3: Automatic metric for reliable optimization and evaluation of machine translation systems. In *Proceed-*

ings of the sixth workshop on statistical machine translation, pages 85–91.

Jacob Devlin, Ming-Wei Chang, Kenton Lee, and Kristina Toutanova. 2018. Bert: Pre-training of deep bidirectional transformers for language understanding. *arXiv preprint arXiv:1810.04805*.

Yimai Fang and Simone Teufel. 2014. A summariser based on human memory limitations and lexical competition. In *Proceedings of the 14th Conference of the European Chapter of the Association for Computational Linguistics*, pages 732–741.

Orhan Firat and Kyunghyn Cho. 2016. Conditional gated recurrent unit with attention mechanism. *https://github.com/nyu-dl/dl4mt-tutorial/blob/master/docs/cgru.pdf*.

David Graff, Junbo Kong, Ke Chen, and Kazuaki Maeda. 2003. English gigaword. *Linguistic Data Consortium, Philadelphia*, 4(1):34.

Kensho Hara, Hirokatsu Kataoka, and Yutaka Satoh. 2018. Can spatiotemporal 3d cnns retrace the history of 2d cnns and imagenet? In *Proceedings of the IEEE conference on Computer Vision and Pattern Recognition*, pages 6546–6555.

Kaiming He, Xiangyu Zhang, Shaoqing Ren, and Jian Sun. 2016. Deep residual learning for image recognition. In *Proceedings of the IEEE conference on computer vision and pattern recognition*, pages 770–778.

Sepp Hochreiter and Jürgen Schmidhuber. 1997. Long short-term memory. *Neural computation*, 9(8):1735–1780.

Zhu JN, Zhang JJ, Li HR, Zong CQ, et al. 2020. Multimodal summarization with guidance of multimodal reference. Association for Computational Linguistics.

Will Kay, Joao Carreira, Karen Simonyan, Brian Zhang, Chloe Hillier, Sudheendra Vijayanarasimhan, Fabio Viola, Tim Green, Trevor Back, Paul Natsev, et al. 2017. The kinetics human action video dataset. *arXiv preprint arXiv:1705.06950*.

Diederik P Kingma and Jimmy Ba. 2014. Adam: A method for stochastic optimization. *arXiv preprint arXiv:1412.6980*.

Walter Kintsch and Teun A Van Dijk. 1978. Toward a model of text comprehension and production. *Psychological review*, 85(5):363.

Haoran Li, Junnan Zhu, Cong Ma, Jiajun Zhang, Chengqing Zong, et al. 2017. Multi-modal summarization for asynchronous collection of text, image, audio and video.

Jindřich Libovický and Jindřich Helcl. 2017. Attention strategies for multi-source sequence-to-sequence learning. In *Proceedings of the 55th Annual Meeting of the Association for Computational Linguistics (Volume 2: Short Papers)*, pages 196–202.

Chin-Yew Lin. 2004. Rouge: A package for automatic evaluation of summaries. In *Text summarization branches out*, pages 74–81.

Yang Liu and Mirella Lapata. 2019. Text summarization with pretrained encoders. In *Proceedings of the 2019 Conference on Empirical Methods in Natural Language Processing and the 9th International Joint Conference on Natural Language Processing (EMNLP-IJCNLP)*, pages 3721–3731.

Abdel-rahman Mohamed. 2014. Deep neural network acoustic models for asr.

Paul Over, Hoa Dang, and Donna Harman. 2007. Duc in context. *Information Processing & Management*, 43(6):1506–1520.

Shruti Palaskar, Jindrich Libovický, Spandana Gella, and Florian Metze. 2019. Multimodal abstractive summarization for how2 videos. *arXiv preprint arXiv:1906.07901*.

Vijayaditya Peddinti, Guoguo Chen, Vimal Manohar, Tom Ko, Daniel Povey, and Sanjeev Khudanpur. 2015. Jhu aspire system: Robust lvcsr with tdnns, ivector adaptation and rnn-lms. In *2015 IEEE Workshop on Automatic Speech Recognition and Understanding (ASRU)*, pages 539–546. IEEE.

Daniel Povey, Arnab Ghoshal, Gilles Boulianne, Lukas Burget, Ondrej Glembek, Nagendra Goel, Mirko Hannemann, Petr Motlicek, Yanmin Qian, Petr Schwarz, et al. 2011. The kaldi speech recognition toolkit. In *IEEE 2011 workshop on automatic speech recognition and understanding*, CONF. IEEE Signal Processing Society.

Michal Rott and Petr Červa. 2016. Speech-to-text summarization using automatic phrase extraction from recognized text. In *International Conference on Text, Speech, and Dialogue*, pages 101–108. Springer.

Alexander M Rush, Sumit Chopra, and Jason Weston. 2015. A neural attention model for abstractive sentence summarization. In *Proceedings of the 2015 Conference on Empirical Methods in Natural Language Processing*, pages 379–389.

Shagan Sah, Sourabh Kulhare, Allison Gray, Subhashini Venugopalan, Emily Prud'Hommeaux, and Raymond Ptucha. 2017. Semantic text summarization of long videos. In *2017 IEEE Winter Conference on Applications of Computer Vision (WACV)*, pages 989–997. IEEE.

Ramon Sanabria, Ozan Caglayan, Shruti Palaskar, Desmond Elliott, Loïc Barrault, Lucia Specia, and Florian Metze. 2018. How2: a large-scale dataset for multimodal language understanding. *arXiv preprint arXiv:1811.00347*.

Abigail See, Peter J Liu, and Christopher D Manning. 2017. Get to the point: Summarization with pointer-generator networks. *arXiv preprint arXiv:1704.04368*.

Kristian Woodsend and Mirella Lapata. 2012. Multiple aspect summarization using integer linear programming. In *Proceedings of the 2012 Joint Conference on Empirical Methods in Natural Language Processing and Computational Natural Language Learning*, pages 233–243. Association for Computational Linguistics.

Junnan Zhu, Haoran Li, Tianshang Liu, Yu Zhou, Jiajun Zhang, Chengqing Zong, et al. 2018. Msmo: multimodal summarization with multimodal output.

Towards End-to-End In-Image Neural Machine Translation

Elman Mansimov[1,*]   **Mitchell Stern**[2,*]
Mia Chen[3]   **Orhan Firat**[3]   **Jakob Uszkoreit**[3]   **Puneet Jain**[3]
[1]New York University, [2]UC Berkeley,[3]Google Research,
[*]Equal Contribution,
mansimov@cs.nyu.edu, mitchell@berkeley.edu

Abstract

In this paper, we offer a preliminary investigation into the task of in-image machine translation: transforming an image containing text in one language into an image containing the same text in another language. We propose an end-to-end neural model for this task inspired by recent approaches to neural machine translation, and demonstrate promising initial results based purely on pixel-level supervision. We then offer a quantitative and qualitative evaluation of our system outputs and discuss some common failure modes. Finally, we conclude with directions for future work.

1   Introduction

End-to-end neural models have emerged in recent years as the dominant approach to a wide variety of sequence generation tasks in natural language processing, including speech recognition, machine translation, and dialog generation, among many others. While highly accurate, these models typically operate by outputting tokens from a predetermined symbolic vocabulary, and require integration into larger pipelines for use in user-facing applications such as voice assistants where neither the input nor output modality is text.

In the speech domain, neural methods have recently been successfully applied to end-to-end speech translation (Jia et al., 2019; Liu et al., 2019; Inaguma et al., 2019), in which the goal is to translate directly from speech in one language to speech in another language. We propose to study the analogous problem of in-image machine translation. Specifically, an image containing text in one language is to be transformed into an image containing the same text in another language, removing the dependency of any predetermined symbolic vocabulary or processing.

Why In-Image Neural Machine Translation ?
In-image neural machine translation is a com-

pelling test-bed for both research and engineering communities for a variety of reasons. Although there are existing commercial products that address this problem such as image translation feature of Google Translate[1] the underlying technical solutions are unknown. By leveraging large amounts of data and compute, end-to-end neural system could potentially improve overall quality of pipelined approaches for image translation. Second, and arguably more importantly, working directly with pixels has the potential to sidestep issues related to vocabularies, segmentation, and tokenization, allowing for the possibility of more universal approaches to neural machine translation, by unifying input and output spaces via pixels.

Text preprocessing and vocabulary construction has been an active research area leading to work on investigating neural machine translation systems operating on subword units (Sennrich et al., 2016), characters (Lee et al., 2017) and even bytes (Wang et al., 2019) and has been highlighted to be one of the major challenges when dealing with many languages simultaneously in multilingual machine translation (Arivazhagan et al., 2019), and cross-lingual natural language understanding (Conneau et al., 2019). Pixels serve as a straightforward way to share vocabulary among all languages at the expense of being a significantly harder learning task for the underlying models.

In this work, we propose an end-to-end neural approach to in-image machine translation that combines elements from recent neural approaches to the relevant sub-tasks in an end-to-end differentiable manner. We provide the initial problem definition and demonstrate promising first qualitative results using only pixel-level supervision on the target side. We then analyze some of the errors

---

[1]blog.google/translate/instant-camera-translation

Proceedings of the First International Workshop on Natural Language Processing Beyond Text, pages 70–74
Online, November 20, 2020. ©2020 Association for Computational Linguistics
http://www.aclweb.org/anthology/W23-20%2d

made by our models, and in the process of doing so uncover a common deficiency that suggests a path forward for future work.

2 Data Generation

To our knowledge, there are no publicly available datasets for the task of in-image machine translation task. Since collecting aligned natural data for in-image translation would be a difficult and costly process, a more practical approach is to bootstrap by generating pairs of rendered images containing sentences from the WMT 2014 German-English parallel corpus. The dataset consists of 4.5M German-English parallel sentence pairs. We use newstest-2013 as a development set. For each sentence pair, we create a minimal web page for the source and target, then render each using Headless Chrome[2] to obtain a pair of images. The text is displayed in a black 16-pixel sans-serif font on a white background inside of a fixed-size 1024x32-pixel frame. For simplicity, all sentences are vertically centered and left-aligned without any line-wrapping. The consistent position and styling of the text in our synthetic dataset represents an ideal scenario for in-image translation, serving as a good test-bed for initial attempts. Later, one could generalize to more realistic settings by varying the location, size, typeface, and perspective of the text and by using non-uniform backgrounds.

3 Model

Our goal is to build a neural model for the in-image translation task that can be trained end-to-end on example image pairs (X^*, Y^*) of height and width H and W using only pixel-level supervision. We evaluate two approaches for this task: convolutional encoder-decoder model and full model that combines soft versions of the traditional pipeline in order to arrive at a modular yet fully differentiable solution.

3.1 Convolutional Baseline

Inspired by the success of convolutional encoder-decoder architectures for medical image segmentation (Ronneberger et al., 2015), we begin with a U-net style convolutional baseline. In this version of the model, the source image X^* is first compressed into a single continuous vector h_{enc} using a convolutional encoder $h_{enc} = \text{enc}(X^*)$.

---

[2]developers.google.com/headless-chrome

Then, the compressed representation is used as the input to a convolutional decoder that aims to predict all target pixels in parallel. Decoder outputs the probabilities of each pixel $p(Y) = \prod_{i=1}^{H} \prod_{j=1}^{W} \text{softmax}(\text{dec}(h_{enc}))$. The convolutional encoder consists of four residual blocks with the dimensions shown in Table 1, and the convolutional decoder uses the same network structure in reverse order, composing a simple encoder-decoder architecture with a representational bottleneck. We threshold the grayscale value of each pixel in the groundtruth output image at 0.5 to obtain a binary black-and-white target, and use a binary cross-entropy loss on the pixels of the model output as our loss function for training.

Dimensions	In	Out	Kernel	Stride
(1024, 32)	3	64	3	1
(1024, 32)	64	128	3	2
(512, 16)	128	128	3	1
(512, 16)	128	256	3	2
(256, 8)	256	256	3	1
(256, 8)	256	512	3	2
(128, 4)	512	512	3	1
(128, 4)	512	512	3	2

Table 1: The parameters of our convolutional encoder network. Each block contains a residual connection from the input to the output. The decoder network uses the same structure in reverse. Dimensions correspond to the size of image. In, out, kernel and stride correspond to conv layer hyperparameters.

In order to solve the proposed task, this baseline must address the combined challenges of recognizing and rendering text at a pixel level, capturing the meaning of a sentence in a single vector as in early sequence-to-sequence models (Sutskever et al., 2014), and performing non-autoregressive translation (Gu et al., 2018). Although the model can sometimes produce the first few words of the output, it is unable to learn much beyond that; see Figure 1 for a representative example.

3.2 Full Model

To better take advantage of the problem structure, we next propose a modular neural model that breaks the problem down into more manageable sub-tasks while still being trainable end-to-end. Intuitively, one would expect a model that can successfully carry out the in-image machine trans-

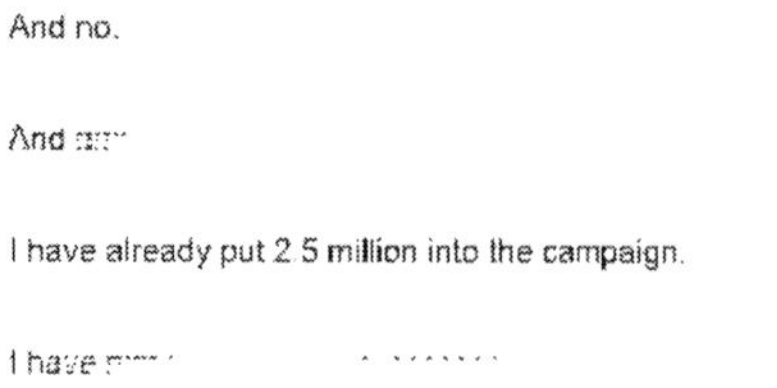

Figure 1: Example predictions made by the baseline convolutional model from Section 3.1. We show two pairs of groundtruth target images followed by generated target images. Although it successfully predicts one or two words, it quickly devolves into noise thereafter.

lation task to first recognize the text represented in the input image, next perform some computation over its internal representation to obtain a soft translation, and finally generate the output image through a learned rendering process. Moreover, just as modern neural machine translation systems predict the output over the span of multiple time steps in a auto-regressive way rather than all at once, it stands to reason that such a decomposition would be of use here as well.

To this end, we propose a revised model that receives as input both the source image X^* and a partial (or proposal) target image $Y^*_{<n}$, applies separate convolutional encoders to each source and target images in order to recognize the text contained therein. The model then applies a self-attention encoder (Vaswani et al., 2017) to the concatenated output of two convolutional encoders to extend the translation by one step, and runs the result through a convolutional decoder. The convolutional decoder is tasked to obtain a new partial output at every generation step, $Y^*_{\leq n}$, that is one step closer to the final target image. The model uses the same structure as the baseline for the convolutional encoder and decoder components, and includes a 6-layer self-attention encoder with hidden dimension 512 and feed-forward dimension 2048 in the middle to help carry out translation within the learned continuous representation space. A visualization of the architecture is given in Figure 2.

With this approach, the problem is decomposed into a sequence of image predictions, each of which conditions on the previously generated output when generating the next candidate output. We use a SentencePiece vocabulary (Kudo and Richardson, 2018) to break the underlying sen-

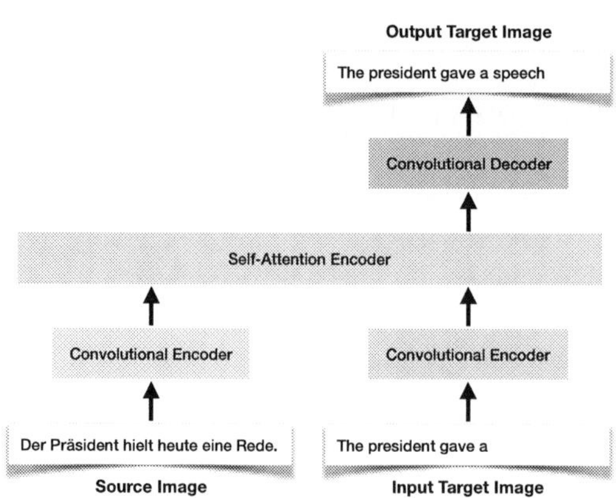

Figure 2: One decoding step for our full model on an example German-English in-image translation pair. The model can be viewed as a fully differentiable analog of the more traditional OCR → translate → render pipeline.

tence into sentence pieces, and decompose each example into one sub-example per sentence piece. The nth sub-example has a target-side input image consisting of the first $n - 1$ sentence pieces, and is trained to predict an output image consisting of the first n sentence pieces from the target sentence. We use the same pixel-level loss as in the baseline. Since the model fully regenerates the output at each step, it must learn to copy the portion that is already present in the target-side input in addition to predicting and rendering the next token. Decoding is done sequentially in a greedy fashion by feeding the model its own predictions (generated partial image) in place of the gold image prefixes.

The use of an external symbolic vocabulary is chosen to speed up the prototyping by making use of existing neural machine translation baselines. The sole purpose is to provide pixel spans that do not cut the characters in half, and simplify the stopping policy. A simple character-based splitting could also be used and/or a stopping policy network could be trained in exchange for increased complexity, and training/inference costs.

4 Results

In Figure 3 we share various source images and corresponding predicted target images generated by the full model. Despite the very high dimensionality of the output, the model occasionally succeeds at predicting the full output translation as shown in Figure 3a. Additionally, Figure 3b shows examples where model makes a minor typo

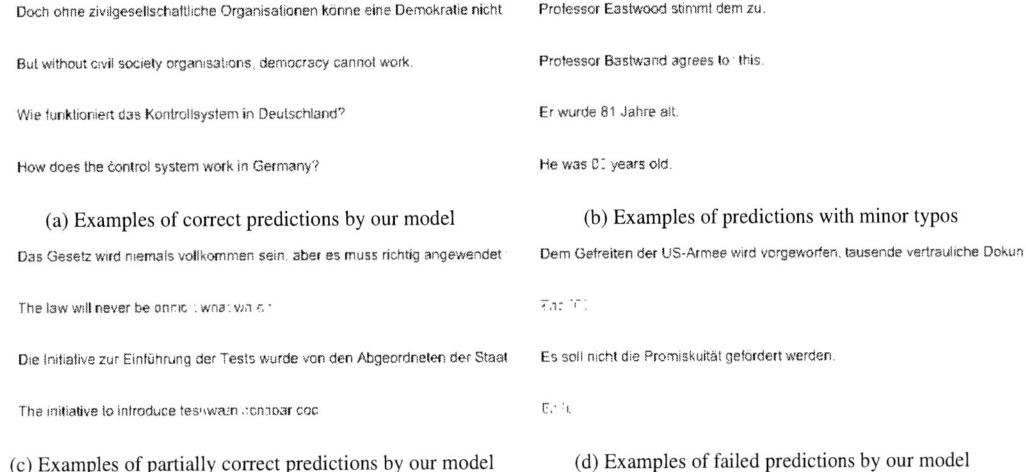

(a) Examples of correct predictions by our model

(b) Examples of predictions with minor typos

(c) Examples of partially correct predictions by our model

(d) Examples of failed predictions by our model

Figure 3: Various types of predictions made by our full model. For more qualitative results please see Appendix.

Figure 4: Analysis of the predictions made by the full model. First row shows the source sentence. Second row shows the groundtruth at the first timestep. Third row shows the probabilities of the pixels predicted by the full model.

	Model	Train Set	Dev Set
NLL	Conv Baseline	0.120	0.117
	Full Model	0.028	**0.025**
BLEU	Conv Baseline	-	0.5
	Full Model	-	**7.7**

Table 2: Per pixel loss function (NLL↓) and generation quality (BLEU↑) of convolutional baseline and full model on WMT'14 German-English Train/Dev sets.

in the earlier proposals and is able to correct itself further during generation process.

Figure 3c and Figure 3d show two major failure modes of our model where it is either able to generate the first part of the sentence and fails to generate the rest or completely fails at generating the image. To better understand the source of errors made by the full model we visualize the probabilities of pixels in Figure 4. We can see that model is uncertain between producing word *However* and *Nevertheless* which leads to artifacts when taking the $\arg\max$ value of each pixel during decoding similar to ones displayed in Figure 3d.

On Table 2 we provide quantitative results of the both models proposed. The full model achieves significantly lower negative log likelihood score compared to convolutional baseline due to an easier task of predicting parts of the image. Neither of the models overfit on the development set. We further quantitatively measure our models by transcribing the generated images into text with a neu-

ral OCR model and measuring the BLEU (Papineni et al., 2002) score. Convolutional baseline fails to produce images that contain transcribed text and is significantly outperformed by our full model in terms of BLEU score.

5 Conclusion

In this paper, we introduce the task of in-image neural machine translation and develop an end-to-end model that shows promising results on learning to translate text through purely pixel-level supervision. By doing so, we demonstrate a viable first step towards applying such models in more natural settings, such as translating texts, menus, or street signs within real-world images. Future work should explore models that do not rely on off-the-shelf text tokenizers to decompose the very hard image generation problem into sequence of simpler image predictions. We hypothesize that discrete latent variables (van den Oord et al., 2017) are best suited to implicitly segment the image and capture the sequential nature of this task.

References

Naveen Arivazhagan, Ankur Bapna, Orhan Firat, Dmitry Lepikhin, Melvin Johnson, Maxim Krikun, Mia Xu Chen, Yuan Cao, George Foster, Colin Cherry, Wolfgang Macherey, Zhifeng Chen, and Yonghui Wu. 2019. Massively multilingual neural machine translation in the wild: Findings and challenges.

Alexis Conneau, Kartikay Khandelwal, Naman Goyal, Vishrav Chaudhary, Guillaume Wenzek, Francisco Guzmn, Edouard Grave, Myle Ott, Luke Zettlemoyer, and Veselin Stoyanov. 2019. Unsupervised cross-lingual representation learning at scale.

Jiatao Gu, James Bradbury, Caiming Xiong, Victor O.K. Li, and Richard Socher. 2018. Nonautoregressive neural machine translation. In *International Conference on Learning Representations*.

Hirofumi Inaguma, Kevin Duh, Tatsuya Kawahara, and Shinji Watanabe. 2019. Multilingual end-to-end speech translation.

Ye Jia, Ron J. Weiss, Fadi Biadsy, Wolfgang Macherey, Melvin Johnson, Zhifeng Chen, and Yonghui Wu. 2019. Direct speech-to-speech translation with a sequence-to-sequence model.

Taku Kudo and John Richardson. 2018. SentencePiece: A simple and language independent subword tokenizer and detokenizer for neural text processing. In *Proceedings of the 2018 Conference on Empirical Methods in Natural Language Processing: System Demonstrations*, pages 66–71, Brussels, Belgium. Association for Computational Linguistics.

Jason Lee, Kyunghyun Cho, and Thomas Hofmann. 2017. Fully character-level neural machine translation without explicit segmentation. In *TACL*.

Yuchen Liu, Hao Xiong, Zhongjun He, Jiajun Zhang, Hua Wu, Haifeng Wang, and Chengqing Zong. 2019. End-to-end speech translation with knowledge distillation.

Aäron van den Oord, Oriol Vinyals, and Koray Kavukcuoglu. 2017. Neural discrete representation learning. In *NIPS*.

Kishore Papineni, Salim Roukos, Todd Ward, and Wei-Jing Zhu. 2002. Bleu: a method for automatic evaluation of machine translation. In *ACL*.

Olaf Ronneberger, Philipp Fischer, and Thomas Brox. 2015. U-net: Convolutional networks for biomedical image segmentation. In *Medical Image Computing and Computer-Assisted Intervention (MICCAI)*, volume 9351 of *LNCS*, pages 234–241. Springer. (available on arXiv:1505.04597 [cs.CV]).

Rico Sennrich, Barry Haddow, and Alexandra Birch. 2016. Neural machine translation of rare words with subword units. In *ACL*.

Ilya Sutskever, Oriol Vinyals, and Quoc V Le. 2014. Sequence to sequence learning with neural networks. In Z. Ghahramani, M. Welling, C. Cortes, N. D. Lawrence, and K. Q. Weinberger, editors, *Advances in Neural Information Processing Systems 27*, pages 3104–3112. Curran Associates, Inc.

Ashish Vaswani, Noam Shazeer, Niki Parmar, Jakob Uszkoreit, Llion Jones, Aidan N Gomez, Ł ukasz Kaiser, and Illia Polosukhin. 2017. Attention is all you need. In I. Guyon, U. V. Luxburg, S. Bengio, H. Wallach, R. Fergus, S. Vishwanathan, and R. Garnett, editors, *Advances in Neural Information Processing Systems 30*, pages 5998–6008. Curran Associates, Inc.

Changhan Wang, Kyunghyun Cho, and Jiatao Gu. 2019. Neural machine translation with byte-level subwords.

Reasoning Over History: Context Aware Visual Dialog

Muhammad A. Shah *
mshah1@cmu.edu

Shikib Mehri*
amehri@cmu.edu

Tejas Srinivasan*
tsriniva@cmu.edu

Language Technologies Institute
Carnegie Mellon University
Pittsburgh, PA

Abstract

While neural models have been shown to exhibit strong performance on single-turn visual question answering (VQA) tasks, extending VQA to a multi-turn, conversational setting remains a challenge. One way to address this challenge is to augment existing strong neural VQA models with the mechanisms that allow them to retain information from previous dialog turns. One strong VQA model is the MAC network, which decomposes a task into a series of attention-based reasoning steps. However, since the MAC network is designed for single-turn question answering, it is not capable of referring to past dialog turns. More specifically, it struggles with tasks that require reasoning over the dialog history, particularly coreference resolution. We extend the MAC network architecture with Context-aware Attention and Memory (CAM), which attends over control states in past dialog turns to determine the necessary reasoning operations for the current question. MAC nets with CAM achieve up to 98.25% accuracy on the CLEVR-Dialog dataset, beating the existing state-of-the-art by 30% (absolute). Our error analysis indicates that with CAM, the model's performance particularly improved on questions that required coreference resolution.

1   Introduction

Visual dialog is the task of answering a sequence of questions about a given image such that responding to any one question in the dialog requires context from the previous dialog history. The task of visual dialog (Das et al., 2017b; Kottur et al., 2019) brings together several fundamental building blocks of intelligent systems: visual understanding, natural language understanding and complex reasoning. The multimodal nature of visual dialog requires approaches that jointly model and reason over both

modalities. Furthermore, visual dialog necessitates the ability to resolve visual coreferences, which arise when two phrases in the dialog refer to the same object in the image. Visual coreference resolution requires both an ability to reason over coreferences in the dialog, as well as ground the entities from the language modality in the visual one.

In contrast to large-scale realistic datasets for visual dialog, such as VisDial (Das et al., 2017b), Kottur et al. (2019) introduce CLEVR-Dialog as a diagnostic dataset for visual dialog. In contrast to other visual dialog datasets, CLEVR-Dialog is synthetically generated - this allows it to be both large-scale and structured in nature. This diagnostic dataset allows for improved fine-grained analysis, using the structured nature of the images and language. This fine-grained analysis allows researchers to study the different components in isolation and identify bottlenecks in end-to-end systems for visual dialog.

Highly structured models have performed well on visual question answering and visual dialog (Andreas et al., 2016b,a; Kottur et al., 2018) by leveraging explicit *program modules* to perform composition reasoning. CorefNMN Kottur et al. (2018), which leverages explicit program modules for coreference resolution, was the previous state-of-the-art model on the CLEVR-Dialog dataset. However, the explicit definition of *program modules* requires handcrafting and limits generalizability. As such, we explore mechanisms of relaxing the structural constrains by using MAC Networks (Hudson and Manning, 2018) and adapting it to the task of dialog. Specifically, we introduce the Context-aware Attention and Memory (CAM) to serve as an inductive bias that allows MAC networks to explicitly capture the necessary context from the dialog history.

CAM consists of a context-aware attention mechanism and a multi-turn memory state. The context-aware attention mechanism attends over the control

---

* equal contribution

75

Proceedings of the First International Workshop on Natural Language Processing Beyond Text, pages 75–83
Online, November 20, 2020. ©2020 Association for Computational Linguistics
http://www.aclweb.org/anthology/W23-20%2d

states of past dialog turns, to determine the control states for the current dialog turn. Since control states in a MAC networks are analogous to program modules, the attention effectively leverages past reasoning operations to inform current reasoning operations. For example, if the MAC network had to locate the *"the red ball"*, a future turn which refers to *"the object to the left of the previous red object"* can attend to the control state responsible for locating the red ball. Meanwhile the multi-turn memory *remembers* information extracted to answer previous questions in the dialog. Similar to the explicit programs of CorefNMN, CAM serves to model properties of dialog (e.g., coreference resolution, history dependent reasoning). However, unlike CorefNMN, CAM does not require explicit handcrafting, can be trained end-to-end and is capable of generalization.

Our methods attain state-of-the-art performance on CLEVR-Dialog, with a **30% improvement** over the prior work. Further, CAM provides strong performance gains over MAC networks across several different experimental setups. Analysis shows that CAM's attention weights are meaningful, and particularly useful for questions that require coreference resolution across dialog turns.

2 Related Work

2.1 Visual Question Answering

Visual Question Answering (VQA) requires models to reason about an image, conditioned on a complex natural language question. Solving VQA requires the ability to reason over images and grounding language entities in the visual modality. There have been several datasets proposed for this task, such as the open-ended VQA (Antol et al., 2015) and diagnostic CLEVR (Johnson et al., 2017) datasets, and several models proposed to solve this task (Yu et al., 2015; Malinowski and Fritz, 2014; Gao et al., 2015; Ren et al., 2015; Liu et al., 2019).

State-of-the-art modeling approaches to VQA can largely be broken into two categories: modular networks (Yi et al., 2018; Andreas et al., 2016b; Hu et al., 2017), and end-to-end differentiable networks (Hudson and Manning, 2018). Neural Module Networks (NMNs) consist of specialized neural modules and can be composed into programs. Since the program construction is not differentiable, training module networks involves complex reinforcement learning training techniques. Moreover, the strong structural constraints along with the need

to handcraft modules limits the generalizability of these models. We think that relaxing some structural constraints, such as those involved in handcrafted models, while retaining other, specifically those that allow for compositional reasoning, would yield powerful yet flexible models.

As a step in this direction, Hudson and Manning (2018) have proposed MAC Networks (Memory, Attention and Comprehension Networks) which simulates a p-step compositional reasoning process by decomposing the question into a series of attention-based reasoning steps. Unlike NMNs, MAC networks do not have specialized program modules, instead they use a control unit to predict a continuous valued vector representation of the reasoning process to be performed at each step.

2.2 Visual Dialog

As models achieve human-level performance on VQA, Das et al. (2017a) and Kottur et al. (2019) proposed to extend them to a conversational setting. Concretely, visual dialog is a multi-turn conversation grounded in an image. In addition to the challenges of VQA, visual dialog requires reasoning over multiple turns of dialog, in which can refer to information introduced in previous dialog turns.

Several datasets have been introduced to study the problem of visual dialog, such as the large-scale VisDial dataset (Das et al., 2017a) and the diagnostic CLEVR-Dialog dataset (Kottur et al., 2019). CLEVR-Dialog is a programmatically constructed dataset with complex images and conversations reasoning about the objects in a given image. Similar to the CLEVR dataset, CLEVR-Dialog comprises of queries and responses about entities in a static image. However, in this multi-turn dataset, queries make references to entities mentioned in previous turns of the dialog, and can thus not be treated as single-turn queries. The main challenge in CLEVR-Dialog is thus visual coreference resolution - resolving multiple references across dialog turns to the same entity in the image.

Several recently proposed methods use reinforcement learning techniques to solve this problem (Strub et al., 2017; Das et al., 2017b). Strub et al. (2017) policy gradient based method for visually grounded task-oriented dialogues. On the other hand, Das et al. (2017b) utilise a goal-driven training for visual question answernig and dialog agents via a cooperative game between two agents (questioner and answerer) and learn the policies of these agents using deep reinforcement learning.

Other approaches utilise transferring knowledge from a discriminatively trained model to a generative dialog model (Lu et al., 2016) and by using differentiable memory to solve visual coreferences (Seo et al., 2017). More specifically, Seo et al. (2017) utilise an associative attention memory for retrieving previous attentions which are most useful for answering the current question. Later, the retrieved attention is combined with a tentative one via dynamic parameter prediction in order to answer the current question.

Kottur et al. (2018) adapted NMNs used in (Andreas et al., 2016b) with an addition of two modules (Refer and Exclude) specifically meant for handling coreference resolution. These two modules perform explicit coreference resoltuion at a word level granularity. The module 'Refer' grounds coreferences in the conversation history while 'Exclude' handles contextual shifts. This Coreference Neural Module Networks (Coref-NMN) were applied to CLEVR-Dialog (Kottur et al., 2019), and achieve the best accuracy on the dataset.

3 Methods

3.1 Problem Statement

Formally, the task we are tackling in this paper is to pick the correct answer, $a_t^* \in \mathcal{A}$ for a question, with representation $q_t \in \mathcal{Q}$, based on an image, $I \in \mathcal{I}$, with a caption, $C \in \mathcal{C}$, and a past dialog history, $\mathcal{H}_t = \{(q_1, a_1), (q_2, a_2)..(q_{t-1}, a_{t-1})\}$, where a_i is the answer to question q_i. In practice, $\mathcal{I}$ does not contain the actual image, but rather, an embedding of the image computed using a pretrained image recognition model.

3.2 MAC Network Architecture

Since our approach builds upon the MAC Network architecture (Hudson and Manning, 2018), we will briefly introduce it in this section before presenting our own novel extensions to it in the subsequent sections.

The MAC network has three core components: the input unit, the MAC cell and the output unit. The input unit computes an image representation, a single question embedding for the entire question and contextualized word embeddings for each word in the question. The output of the input unit is recurrently passed through the MAC cell p times, where p is a predefined hyper-parameter. Each pass through the MAC cell is meant to simulate one step

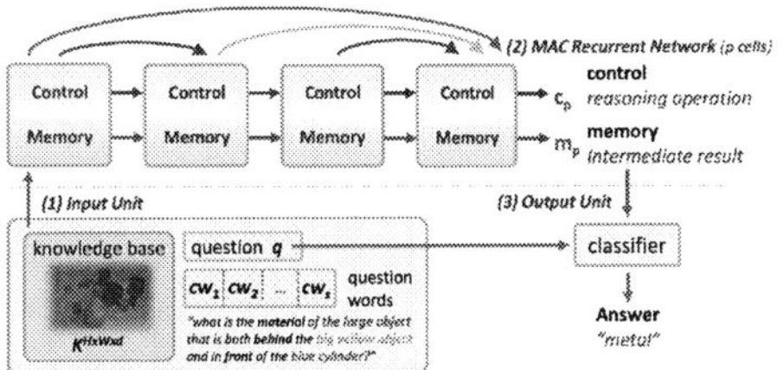

Figure 1: The MAC Network Architecture (image from (Hudson and Manning, 2018))

of a p-step reasoning process. The MAC cell consists of three sub-modules, namely the control, read and write units and a running memory state that accumulates the results of each reasoning step. The control unit computes an embedding for the ith reasoning operation based on the $(i-1)^{\text{th}}$ reasoning operation, and the sentence and word embeddings of the question. The read unit attends on the image representation using the current memory state and the output of the control unit, to extract the information required for current reasoning step. The write unit uses the output of the read unit to update the memory state. After p reasoning steps have been performed, the output unit uses the memory state to predict the answer. It is assumed in the architecture that the answers are categorical. This process is illustrated in Figure 1.

3.3 Extending MAC Network With CAM

Since the MAC network is designed to answer single-turn questions, it is not able to answer questions that rely on context established in previous turns of a dialog. In this section we describe our proposed Context-aware Attention and Memory (CAM) mechanism that endows MAC networks with the ability to perform multi-turn reasoning by *remembering* the reasoning steps it performed, and the information it extracted from the image to answer questions posed in past turns. CAM has two components, namely a memory state that remains persistent across multiple turns and an attention mechanism that encodes contextual information from past turns in the current control state.

3.3.1 Multi-Turn Memory

The first extension we propose endows the model with a memory that remains persistent across dialog turns. Specifically, we want to allow the model to *remember* the information it has already extracted from the image in earlier dialog turns, so that it can use this information to answer context-dependent questions in subsequent turns.

To implement this memory mechanism we leverage the existing memory state of MAC networks, with a slight modification. In the original MAC network architecture the memory state is initialized with a zero vector for each question, and is updated after each of the p reasoning steps before being discarded. Formally, the memory state at the kth reasoning step of the tth turn in the dialog is computed as

$$m_k^{(t)} = \begin{cases} f(I_k^{(t)}, \mathbf{0}), & k = 0 \\ f(I_k^{(t)}, m_{k-1}^{(t)}), & k > 0 \end{cases} \quad (1)$$

where $I_k^{(t)}$ represents the information extracted from the image and f is a function that computes the updated memory state. Under this scheme, the information accumulated while reasoning about the first question in the dialog is discarded when the model starts reasoning about the second question. In our implementation we initialize the memory once for each dialog, and retain it across all the turns of the dialog. Formally, this leads to the modification of Equation 1 to

$$m_k^{(t)} = \begin{cases} f(I_k^{(t)}, \mathbf{0}), & t = 0, k = 0 \\ f(I_k^{(t)}, m_k^{(t-1)}), & t > 0, k = 0 \\ f(I_k^{(t)}, m_{k-1}^{(t)}), & k > 0 \end{cases} \quad (2)$$

3.3.2 Context-aware Attention Mechanism

For our second extension, we propose to allow the model to *recall* previous control states when computing the current control state. The intuition behind this extension is that if the current question, q_t, references an entity from a previous question, q_{t-k} or its answer, the reasoning steps for answering q_t are likely to be similar, to those for answering q_{t-k}, at least insofar as they relate to the coreferent entity. Since the introduction of the coreferent entity was more recent with respect to q_{t-k}, compared to q_t, it would have been more salient in the model's memory. Therefore, it is likely that the model would have applied appropriate reasoning processes in when answering q_{t-k}. At q_t, the coreferent entity is less salient in the model's memory, which increases the likelihood of the model selecting the inappropriate reasoning steps.

To mitigate the aforementioned problem and explicitly incorporate the dialog context into the model, we introduce a transformer-like self-attention mechanism on the previous control states.

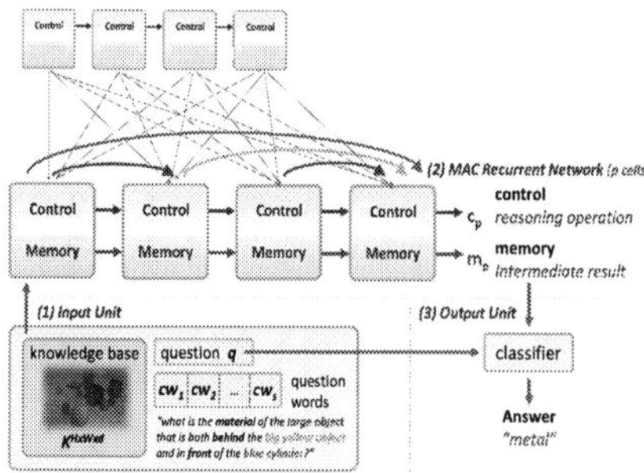

Figure 2: The modified MAC Network architecture which explicitly incorporates dialog context

The resulting architecture is illustrated in Figure 2. This mechanism allow the model to *explicitly* attend to the past outputs of the control unit, both, from previous reasoning steps in the current turn and the reasoning steps from the previous dialog turns, while computing the control output for the current reasoning step.

Concretely, given the unattended control representations, $\mathbf{C} = [c_1^{(1)}...c_{i-1}^{(t)}]^T$ of all the reasoning steps until the ith reasoning step of turn t, the final control output, $\bar{\mathbf{C}}$, is computed as the *fusion* (Hu et al., 2017) of the attended control representation, $\hat{\mathbf{C}}$, and the unattended control representation as follows:

$$E = \phi_{key}(\mathbf{C})\phi_{key}(\mathbf{C})^T \quad (3)$$
$$A = \text{softmax}(\text{tril}(E)) \quad (4)$$
$$\bar{\mathbf{C}} = fusion(\mathbf{C}, A\mathbf{C}) \quad (5)$$

where ϕ_{key} and ϕ_{value} represent the key and value projections used in the self-attention step, $\text{tril}(E)$ represents the matrix obtained by setting the values in the upper triangle of E to zero and the *fusion* module is defined as follows:

$$fusion(x, y) = g\tilde{x} + (1 - g)x$$
$$\tilde{x} = relu(W_r[x]; y; x \odot y; x - y)$$
$$g = sigmoid(W_g[x]; y; x \odot y; x - y)$$

where $\odot$ represents element-wise multiplication.

4 Experimental Setup

4.1 Dataset

The CLEVR-Dialog dataset[1] (Kottur et al., 2019), pictured in Figure 3, consists of several modali-

[1]https://github.com/satwikkottur/clevr-dialog

78

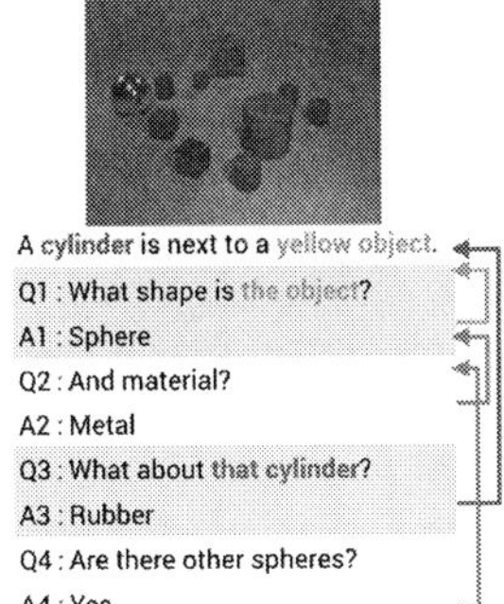

Figure 3: Example from the CLEVR-Dialog dataset, consisting of an image, a dialog. Each dialog begins with a caption describing the image, followed by a round of questions and answers. Each question relies on information from previous dialog turns.

ties: visual images, natural language dialog and structured scene graphs.

Each image I and its respective complete scene graph S_a depicts a scene containing several objects. Each object has four major attributes, enumerated as follows:

- Color – *blue, brown, cyan, gray, green, purple, red, yellow*

- Shape – *cylinder, cube, sphere*

- Size – *large, small*

- Material – *metal, rubber*

Every pair of objects has a spatial relationship which describes their relative spatial position: *front, back, right, left*.

Each dialog is an interaction between a Questioner and an Answerer. The Answerer, who has the image and the complete scene graph, begins by providing a caption that describes the image. The Questioner, who does not see the image, aims to build up a complete scene graph by repeatedly asking questions. As the Questioner gets more information, they build up a partial scene graph S_q^t. Though, during data collection the Answerer had a complete scene graph, during the task of visual dialog – the scene graph should not be used during testing and the Answerer can only use the image.

Each dialog consists of 10 turns. Questions are generated with the use of 23 question templates, which can be grouped into several categories: **Count** questions which ask for the number of objects that satisfy certain conditions, **Existence**

questions are yes/no questions that query about certain conditions in the image and **Seek** questions ask for attributes of certain objects. The seek question type is 60% of the dataset, followed by count at 23% and exist at 17%. There are 29 unique answers (e.g., 'yes', 'no', 'blue', '1', '2' etc.), with all the answers being single-word.

A strong motivation of the CLEVR-Dialog dataset is to model *dialog* in the context of an image. To this end, there are two types of history dependancy. The first is coreference, wherein a phrase in a question refers to an earlier referent in the history. The mean coreference distance is 3.2 turns and the distance spans between 1-10 turns. The second type of history dependency is when the question relies on the entire dialog history, rather than a specific referent. For example: *'How many other objects are there?'*

The dataset has $85k$ unique images, with 5 dialogs per image for a total of $425k$ dialogs. Each dialog consists of a caption, and ten turns of question-answer pairs, for a total of $4.25M$ questions and answers. There are 23 unique question templates and $73k$ unique questions.

Since CLEVR-dialog has 29 unique single-word answers, the metric used is accuracy. The structured nature of the dataset allows for accuracy breakdown by coreference distance and question type, as shown by Kottur et al. (2019).

4.2 Implementation Details

All models were implemented in PyTorch [2] building on an open source implementation of MAC networks. While training history agnostic models each dialog turn was treated as an independent question and in each iteration we trained the model on 128 random dialog turns. Meanwhile, we trained the context-aware models by providing them one dialog turn at a time, with a batch size of 12 dialogs (120 turns). The learning rate and the number of reasoning steps for the MAC networks was set to `2e-4` and 8, respectively.

Since CLEVR-Dialog consists of only a training set and a development set, the development set was used for evaluation. We remove 1000 images and their respective dialogs from the training set to use for validation, for a total of 5000 dialogs and 50,000 dialog turns. The models were set to trained for 25 epochs but if the validation accuracy

---

[2] `https://github.com/tohinz/` `pytorch-mac-network`

Model	CQ	CAA	MTM	Accuracy (%)
NMN	-	-	-	56.6
CorefNMN	-	-	-	68.0
MAC Networks	✗	✗	✗	65.9
	✗	✓	✗	89.43*
	✗	✓	✓	97.98*
	✓	✗	✗	98.08*
	✓	✓	✓	98.16†
	✓	✓	✗	98.25*

Table 1: Performance of our baseline models, and the effect of our dialog-specific augmentations, namely Concatetating Questions (CQ), Context-Aware Attention (CAA) and Multi-Turn Memory (MTM), to the MAC network (Hudson and Manning, 2018).
$^*p < 0.00001$ compared with previous row.
$^†p < 0.001$ compared with previous row.

does not increase for 5 epochs, we stop training so some models were trained for 16-17 epochs while others were trained for 25. We ran experiments on a cluster with 32 core Intel Xenon processors and Nvidia 1080Ti GPUs.

4.3 Baselines

We use Neural Module Networks (Andreas et al., 2016b) (NMN) and CorefNMN (Kottur et al., 2018) as our baslines because the dataset paper (Kottur et al., 2019) reports them to have the best performance on CLEVR dialog.

Neural Module Networks (NMN) proposed by Andreas et al. (2016b) are a general class of recursive neural networks (Socher et al., 2013) which provide a framework for constructing deep networks with dynamic computational structure. NMNs are history agnostic, making them a weak baseline for this dataset.

CorefNMNs (Kottur et al., 2018) adapts NMNs (Andreas et al., 2016b) with an addition of two modules (Refer and Exclude) that perform explicit coreference resolution at a word level granularity. 'Refer' grounds coreferences in the conversation history while 'Exclude' handles contextual shifts.

5 Results

In Table 1, we examine the performance of our baseline models, and the effect of Context-aware Attention Mechanism (CAM). We experiment with three different combinations of our dialog-specific extensions to the MAC network architecture:

(i) context-aware attention over control states,
(ii) multi-turn memory, and
(iii) concatenating the dialog history as input to MAC - an obvious but naive and inefficient

strategy for incorporating contextual information into a single-turn QA model.

When none of these three extensions are present, we obtain the vanilla MAC network which does not have the ability to reason over the dialog context. We see that vanilla MAC achieves 10% higher accuracy than NMN, which is also history-agnostic, and is surprisingly close to CorefNMN, which explicitly reasons over the dialog history. The fact that a single turn model can correctly answer two-thirds of the questions in a very large dataset raises some concerns regarding how representative is the dataset of an actual dialog task. Adding context-aware attention to the MAC improves the accuracy of the model considerably to 89.43%. Introducing multi-turn memory to this model yields an accuracy of 97.98% accuracy - an improvement of 30% (absolute) on the performance of vanilla MAC network and benchmark CorefNMN. These results emphatically establish the efficacy of CAM and establish a new state-of-the-art for CLEVR-Dialog.

Perhaps most notably, concatenating the dialog history to the current query works remarkably well for MAC networks, achieving 98.08% accuracy with no other augmentations to the MAC network. Introducing context-aware attention further improves accuracy to 98.25%, which yet again evidences the efficacy of the attention mechanism we propose. However, introducing the multi-turn memory results in a slight decrease in performance, indicating that the memory mechanism is not useful when the entire dialog context is present.

We think it is important to mention here that, concatenating the dialog history is a naive method, and this method becomes computationally inefficient when the dialog history is longer and the questions themselves are longer. While it is true that the context aware attention mechanism also stores additional data - the past control states. However, since the control states are fixed sized, the additional memory and computation required is in $O(Tp)$, where T is the maximum number of dialog turns and p is the number of reasoning steps to be performed. On the other hand, the increase memory and computation requirements for concatenation is in $O(|Q_{max}|Tp)$ where $|Q_{max}|$ is the length of the longest question. Without concatenating the dialog history, incorporating the multi-turn memory greatly improves accuracy (89.43% → 97.98%), while being more computationally efficient.

These results indicate that relaxing the structure

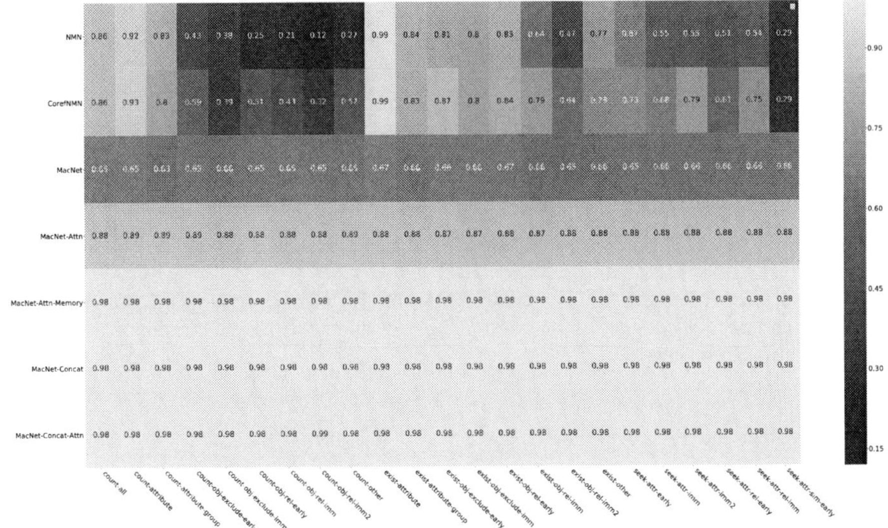

Figure 4: Breakdown of the accuracies of the models by question type. Different question types require different reasoning, especially pertaining to the dialog history.

of the model by eliminating hand-crafted modules gives the model much more flexibility in how it processes the input query, allowing it to perform more complex reasoning than the programs assembled by Neural Module Networks.

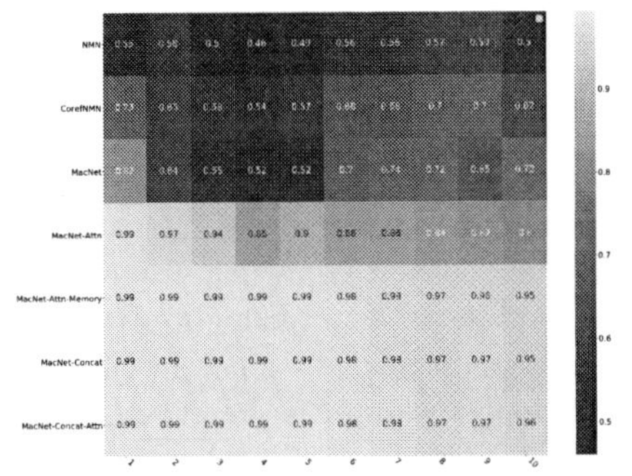

Figure 5: Breakdown of the accuracies of different models on different turns in the dialog

6 Analysis

6.1 Performance Breakdown

In order to better understand the results presented above, we breakdown the accuracy of the models along dialog turns and question types.

6.1.1 Question Types and Accuracy

The heatmap shown in Figure 4 breaks down the accuracies of the models for different question types.

Different question types require different reasoning about the image and the dialog. For example, `count-obj-rel-*` requires the models to count the number of objects *relative* to another entity, often one that was discussed earlier in the dialog. We observe that MacNet-Concat-Attn obtains a 1% gain over MacNet-Concat and MacNet-Attn-Memory for the `count-obj-rel-imm2` question type, which requires reasoning about the number of objects relative to one from earlier in the dialog. These question types are follow-ups (e.g., "*how about to it's left*"), meaning that they have both anaphora and ellipsis. As such the performance gains on this question type are indicative of better dialog modelling. It is important to note that the above question types are also the ones that have the lowest performance across all models. This highlights the importance of developing specialized strategies for modelling dialog.

6.1.2 Dialog Turn Number and Accuracy

The heatmap shown in Figure 5 presents the accuracy of the models when answering questions at different dialog turns. MacNet-Attn performs significantly better than MacNet. The fact that MacNet-Attn performs better at later turns suggests that the model is effectively resolving coreferences from the dialog history. Likewise, MacNet-Attn-Memory obtains even stronger performance gains, especially at later dialog turns. In the final turn of dialogs, MacNet-Attn-Memory is 15% more accu-

Previous Turns	There are 4 small things. What is the number of green things in the view, if present?	
	Are there other things that share its color in the scene?	
	If there is a thing in front of the above green thing, what is its material?	
Current Turn	If there is a thing to the right of it, what color is it?	
Previous Turns	The image has a yellow thing right of a cylinder. How many other things are in the picture?	
	What is the size of the previous cylinder?	
	Does the previous yellow thing have things to its behind?	
Current Turn	If there is a thing behind the previous cylinder, what is its material?	

Table 2: Dialog examples where attention over control states of previous dialog turns informs the model of which previous turn is important to attend to when answering the current query (the last question of the dialog). Darker shade means higher attention weight.

rate than MacNet-Attn and 23% over MacNet.

MacNet-Concat-Attn obtains a 1% improvement over MacNet-Attn-Memory and MacNet-Concat, at the 9th and 10th dialog turns, respectively. This performance gain is relatively smaller, however, since the accuracies are so high, the relative error reduction is still significant. It is important to note that a 1% improvement in accuracy corresponds to answering 7500 more questions correctly.

6.2 Attention Analysis

We verify that the context-aware attention over the control states is performing coreference resolution by looking at the attention weights assigned to each past question in the dialog history. Since 8 control states are computed per question, we consider the maximum attention weight between any control state of the current question and any control state in the past question.

Table 2 presents examples of turn-level attention weights for two different dialogs (in red and blue, respectively). The first example shows that a higher attention weight is allotted to the immediately preceding dialog turn. We note that this preceding turn contains a reference to the entity which is referred to in the current turn.

In the second example, we see that a much higher attention is given to the first turn (which includes the image caption). We noticed that lots of dialog turns give a higher attention to the first dialog turn. This could be because a lot of questions start a new line of dialog by making a reference back to the original image caption. For instance, in the current turn, a question is asked about an entity in relation to the cylinder which is mentioned in the caption.

These examples illustrate that CAM is able to identify the referent turn in the dialog and appropriately attend to it.

7 Conclusion

We present Context-aware Attention and Memory (CAM), a set of dialog-specific augmentations to MAC networks (Hudson and Manning, 2018). CAM consists of a context-aware attention mechanism which attends over the MAC control states of past dialog turns and a persistent, multi-turn memory which is accumulated over multiple turns of the dialog. These augmentations serve as an inductive bias that allow the architecture to capture various important properties of dialog, such as coreference and history dependency.

Our methods attain state-of-the-art performance on CLEVR-Dialog, with our best model attaining an accuracy of **98.25%**, a **30% improvement** over all prior results. Further, CAM attains strong performance gains over vanilla MAC networks, especially for question types that require coreference resolution and later dialog turns. Ablation experiments indicate that both of the components in CAM provide significant improvement in performance. We also verified that the context aware attention mechanism in indeed captures coreferences between the dialog turns.

Our results are indicative of the flexibility of weakly structured models, like MAC networks and their ability to adapt to different problem settings. To adapt MAC networks for visual dialog we had to devise a mechanism to provide it with contextual information from past turns. Thereafter, the other components of the model were able to adapt and use this information to improve performance on the task, whereas to adapt NMN to visual dialog Kottur et al. (2018) had to devise specialized modules to handle specific types of questions.

References

Jacob Andreas, Marcus Rohrbach, Trevor Darrell, and Dan Klein. 2016a. Learning to compose neural networks for question answering. *arXiv preprint arXiv:1601.01705*.

Jacob Andreas, Marcus Rohrbach, Trevor Darrell, and Dan Klein. 2016b. Neural module networks. In *Proceedings of the IEEE Conference on Computer Vision and Pattern Recognition*, pages 39–48.

Stanislaw Antol, Aishwarya Agrawal, Jiasen Lu, Margaret Mitchell, Dhruv Batra, C Lawrence Zitnick, and Devi Parikh. 2015. Vqa: Visual question answering. In *Proceedings of the IEEE international conference on computer vision*, pages 2425–2433.

Abhishek Das, Satwik Kottur, Khushi Gupta, Avi Singh, Deshraj Yadav, José MF Moura, Devi Parikh, and Dhruv Batra. 2017a. Visual dialog. In *Proceedings of the IEEE Conference on Computer Vision and Pattern Recognition*, pages 326–335.

Abhishek Das, Satwik Kottur, José MF Moura, Stefan Lee, and Dhruv Batra. 2017b. Learning cooperative visual dialog agents with deep reinforcement learning. In *Proceedings of the IEEE International Conference on Computer Vision*, pages 2951–2960.

Haoyuan Gao, Junhua Mao, Jie Zhou, Zhiheng Huang, Lei Wang, and Wei Xu. 2015. Are you talking to a machine? dataset and methods for multilingual image question. In *Advances in neural information processing systems*, pages 2296–2304.

Ronghang Hu, Jacob Andreas, Marcus Rohrbach, Trevor Darrell, and Kate Saenko. 2017. Learning to reason: End-to-end module networks for visual question answering. In *Proceedings of the IEEE International Conference on Computer Vision*, pages 804–813.

Drew A Hudson and Christopher D Manning. 2018. Compositional attention networks for machine reasoning. *arXiv preprint arXiv:1803.03067*.

Justin Johnson, Bharath Hariharan, Laurens van der Maaten, Li Fei-Fei, C Lawrence Zitnick, and Ross Girshick. 2017. Clevr: A diagnostic dataset for compositional language and elementary visual reasoning. In *Proceedings of the IEEE Conference on Computer Vision and Pattern Recognition*, pages 2901–2910.

Satwik Kottur, José MF Moura, Devi Parikh, Dhruv Batra, and Marcus Rohrbach. 2018. Visual coreference resolution in visual dialog using neural module networks. In *Proceedings of the European Conference on Computer Vision (ECCV)*, pages 153–169.

Satwik Kottur, José MF Moura, Devi Parikh, Dhruv Batra, and Marcus Rohrbach. 2019. Clevr-dialog: A diagnostic dataset for multi-round reasoning in visual dialog. *arXiv preprint arXiv:1903.03166*.

Runtao Liu, Chenxi Liu, Yutong Bai, and Alan L Yuille. 2019. Clevr-ref+: Diagnosing visual reasoning with referring expressions. In *Proceedings of the IEEE Conference on Computer Vision and Pattern Recognition*, pages 4185–4194.

Jiasen Lu, Jianwei Yang, Dhruv Batra, and Devi Parikh. 2016. Hierarchical question-image co-attention for visual question answering. In *Advances In Neural Information Processing Systems*, pages 289–297.

Mateusz Malinowski and Mario Fritz. 2014. A multi-world approach to question answering about real-world scenes based on uncertain input. In *Advances in neural information processing systems*, pages 1682–1690.

Mengye Ren, Ryan Kiros, and Richard Zemel. 2015. Exploring models and data for image question answering. In *Advances in neural information processing systems*, pages 2953–2961.

Paul Hongsuck Seo, Andreas Lehrmann, Bohyung Han, and Leonid Sigal. 2017. Visual reference resolution using attention memory for visual dialog. In *Advances in neural information processing systems*, pages 3719–3729.

Richard Socher, Alex Perelygin, Jean Wu, Jason Chuang, Christopher D Manning, Andrew Ng, and Christopher Potts. 2013. Recursive deep models for semantic compositionality over a sentiment treebank. In *Proceedings of the 2013 conference on empirical methods in natural language processing*, pages 1631–1642.

Florian Strub, Harm De Vries, Jeremie Mary, Bilal Piot, Aaron Courville, and Olivier Pietquin. 2017. End-to-end optimization of goal-driven and visually grounded dialogue systems. *arXiv preprint arXiv:1703.05423*.

Kexin Yi, Jiajun Wu, Chuang Gan, Antonio Torralba, Pushmeet Kohli, and Josh Tenenbaum. 2018. Neural-symbolic vqa: Disentangling reasoning from vision and language understanding. In *Advances in Neural Information Processing Systems*, pages 1031–1042.

Licheng Yu, Eunbyung Park, Alexander C Berg, and Tamara L Berg. 2015. Visual madlibs: Fill in the blank image generation and question answering. *arXiv preprint arXiv:1506.00278*.

Association for Computational Linguistics
209 N. Eighth Street
Stroudsburg, Pennsylvania 18360

ISBN 978-1-7138-1999-8